JOSHUA FIELD

AN ILLUSTRATED FIELD GUIDE
TO THE ELEMENTS & PRINCIPLES
OF ART + DESIGN

FIRST EDITION

Printed in the United States of America

Publisher's Cataloging-in-Publication data
Field, Joshua.
An Illustrated Field Guide to the Elements & Principles of Art + Design / Joshua Field.
p. cm.
ISBN 979-8-218-23153-8

www.joshuafield.com

First Edition

CONTENTS

LIST OF ILLUSTRATIONS

18. Winslow Homer, *Shooting the Rapids*, Saguenay River, 1905-10. Oil on canvas with chalk. Photo courtesy Metropolitan Museum of Art (Gift of Charles S. Homer, 1911). Page 33. Elements: Color.

19. Unknown, *Wall Design - Asistencia of San Antonio de Pala From the Portfolio: "Decorative Art of Spanish California"*, 20th Century. Screenprint on paperboard. Photo courtesy National Gallery of Art (Index of American Design). Page 38. Principles: Balance.

20. Samuel H. Gottscho, *1939 New York World's Fair, Entrance to Perisphere*, ca. 1939. Gelatin silver print. Photo courtesy Metropolitan Museum of Art (Ford Motor Company Collection, Gift of Ford Motor Company and John C. Waddell, 1987). Page 40. Principles: Proportion.

21. John Henry Amschewitz, *The Refugees*, ca. 1906. Wash on cardboard. Photo courtesy Metropolitan Museum of Art (Gift of Spencer Bickerton, 1933). Page 42. Principles: Contrast.

22. Paul Cézanne, *Still Life with Milk Jug and Fruit*, ca. 1900. Oil on Canvas. Photo courtesy National Gallery of Art (Gift of the W. Averell Harriman Foundation in memory of Marie N. Harriman). Page 44. Principles: Repetition.

23. Unknown (Detroit Photographic Co.), *A Monday Washing*, New York City, 1900. Photochrom. Photo courtesy National Gallery of Art (Gift of Mary and Dan Solomon). Page 46. Principles: Rhythm.

24. Louis Comfort Tiffany, *Design for Skylight Window*, 1902–32. Watercolor, gouache, ink, and graphite on artist board. Photo courtesy Metropolitan Museum of Art (Purchase, Walter Hoving and Julia T. Weld Gifts and Dodge Fund, 1967). Page 48. Principles: Pattern.

25. Claude Monet, *The Green Wave*, 1866-67. Oil on canvas. Photo courtesy Metropolitan Museum of Art (H. O. Havemeyer Collection, Bequest of Mrs. H. O. Havemeyer, 1929). Page 50. Principles: Movement.

26. Rembrandt van Rijn, *The Mill*, 1645/1648. Oil on Canvas. Photo courtesy National Gallery of Art (Widener Collection). Page 52. Principles: Emphasis.

27. Childe Hassam, *Surf, Isle of Shoals*, 1913. Oil on Canvas. Photo courtesy National Gallery of Art (Gift of Dr. and Mrs. Sheldon C. Sommers, 1996). Page 54. Principles: Unity.

28. Vasily Kandinsky, *Kleine Welten I (Small Worlds I)*, 1922. Lithograph. Photo courtesy Metropolitan Museum of Art (Harris Brisbane Dick Fund, 1931). Page 56. Principles: Variety.

29. Charles Demuth, *I Saw the Figure 5 in Gold*, 1928. Oil, graphite, Ink and gold leaf on paperboard. Photo courtesy Metropolitan Museum of Art (Alfred Stieglitz Collection, 1949). Page 60. Exercises: Motion and Sound.

30. Jonas Lie, *The Conquerors (Culebra Cut, Panama Canal)*, 1913. Oil on Cavnas. Photo courtesy Metropolitan Museum of Art (George A. Hearn Fund, 1914). Page 62. Exercises: Monumental.

31. Jean Auguste Dominique Ingres, *Joséphine-Éléonore-Marie-Pauline de Galard de Brassac de Béarn (1825–1860), Princesse de Broglie*, 1851-53. Oil on Canvas. Photo courtesy Metropolitan Museum of Art (Robert Lehman Collection, 19764). Page 5. Exercises: Creating Opulence.

32. Alfred Stieglitz, *Georgia O'Keeffe — Neck*, 1921. Palladium Print. Photo courtesy Metropolitan Museum of Art (Gift of Georgia O'Keeffe, through the generosity of The Georgia O'Keeffe Foundation and Jennifer and Joseph Duke, 1997). Page 66. Exercises: Passion and Desire.

33. Henri de Toulouse-Lautrec, *Aristide Bruant, at His Cabaret*, 1893. Four color lithograph. Photo courtesy Metropolitan Museum of Art (Jacques and Natasha Gelman Collection, 1998). Page 68. Exercises: The Power to Captivate.

INTRODUCTION

The taxonomic system known as the elements and principles of art and design has served as an analytical and creative touchstone for generations of artists and designers. The first iteration of the curriculum was introduced by Johannes Itten for his preliminary course at the Bauhaus, a post-war school founded by Walter Gropius who said, "Our guiding principle was that design is neither an intellectual nor a material affair, but simply an integral part of the stuff of life, necessary for everyone in a civilized society."

Unlike the traditional academy model which emphasized the study of narrative and allegory found in old master works, the Bauhaus *Vorkurs* introductory course stressed comprehensive aesthetic systems and focused on creative form. This mode of creation was ideally suited to the nascent but rapidly expanding modernist movement which emphasized the formal aspects of art and design. Bauhaus faculty later fled Nazi Germany to teach at influential American institutions like Harvard and Yale, and in the case of Josef Albers, founded the Black Mountain School. The migration introduced a generation of American artists to the Bauhaus aesthetic system. While the formalist inclinations of modernism were evident in movement offshoots like minimalism and op-art, many postmodern artists began to engage in more pluralistic modes of creative practice.

Some who railed against the formalities of the Bauhaus model early in their careers later realized how critical it had been to their development. For example, as a student at the Black Mountain School, Robert Rauschenberg had a famously contentious relationship with founder and teacher Josef Albers. Reflecting on his experience Rauschenberg said that he found Albers' criticism "so excruciating and so devastating" that he never asked for it. Later in his career he considered Albers the most important teacher that he ever had.

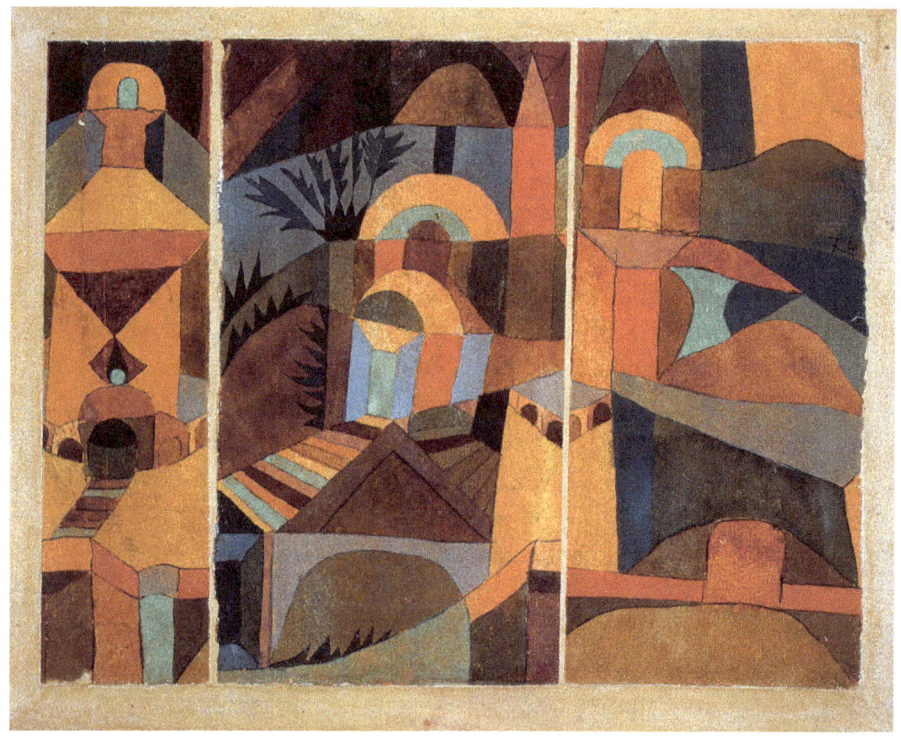

1. Paul Klee, *Temple Gardens*, 1920. Klee taught classes in elemental design theory as part of the Bauhaus preliminary course

Understandably, the rigorous and sometimes tedious work of studying the elements and principles can feel antithetical to the impulse for self expression that often leads students to the study of art. In my own foundational studies, the excitement of assembling small, precise collages of Color-Aid paper in order to replicate Joseph Albers' color paintings quickly gave way to a desire to make something that allowed room for my own voice. The evidence of the exercises' efficacy was only revealed later when the comprehension of color interaction was deployed in the service of personal expression. It was this same application of the elements and principles to the realm of personal expression that brought Rauschenberg back to the fundamentals.

As other artists sought to move beyond the commercial paradigm of the 1980's art world and embrace forms like video and performance that defied commercial exploitation, the elements and principles of art and design found new life working in consort *with* narrative and individual expression rather than against it. Many artists who once resisted the rigorous strictures of the Bauhaus-derived aesthetic system embraced it in order to more purposefully create imagery that worked both on a conscious and subconscious level.

Despite a sometimes tumultuous relationship with the formality of systematized aesthetics, a core of artists, designers, and academics have consistently embraced of the elements and principles of art and design for the purpose of image analysis in both formal critique and self reflection. In the classroom, the elements and principles of art and design continue to be a staple of art education and are now frequently integrated as a tool for visual communication and a scaffold for narrative and experimentation rather than an end unto themselves. This book examines not just the formal structure of the model but ultimately explores the effect that deploying each element and principle can have on a composition and ultimately on the viewer. ■●▲

ABOUT THE AUTHOR

Joshua Field is an nationally and internationally exhibited artist, award-winning graphic designer, and Assistant Professor of Foundations and Fine Arts at the Rocky Mountain College of Art + Design in Denver, CO. He holds a BFA from the Maryland Institute College of Art in Baltimore, MD and an MFA from the University of Massachusetts at Amherst in Amherst, MA. His work has been featured in numerous publications including ArtSlant, DailyCandy DesignYouTrust, and Saatchi Online's 100 Curators / 100 Days , is held in both public and private collections, and can be seen on-line at www.joshuafield.com.

PART ONE

THE ELEMENTS
THE BUILDING BLOCKS OF COMPOSITION

THE BUILDING BLOCKS
OF ART + DESIGN

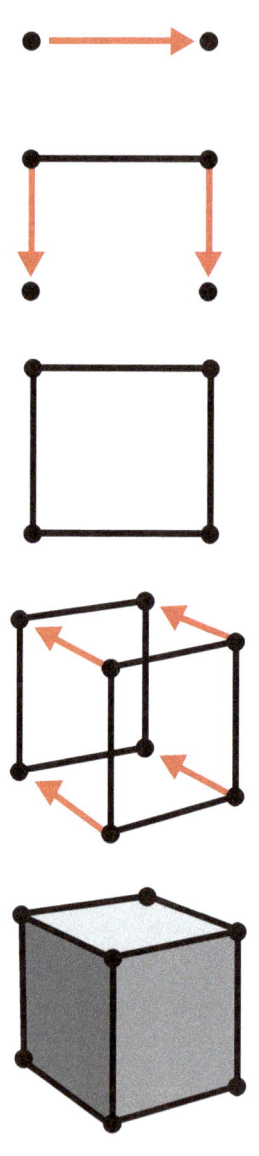

THE ELEMENTS OF ART + DESIGN

The word "composition" is defined in the Oxford English Dictionary as, "The nature of something's ingredients or constituents; the way in which a whole or mixture is made up." For the purposes of visual composition, we can think of the elements of art and design as the ingredients or constituents of an image. I often imagine the elements as the ingredients in a powerful potion that can alter a viewer's perception when added to the brew in specific ways.

The elements serve as building blocks, both for the composition as a whole and often for one another. For example, a point on its own is only a point, but when placed near another point it creates an imaginary or implied line between the two. Picture a "connect the dots" puzzle from your childhood where each dot establishes the vertex of a line, coming together to eventually form a shape.

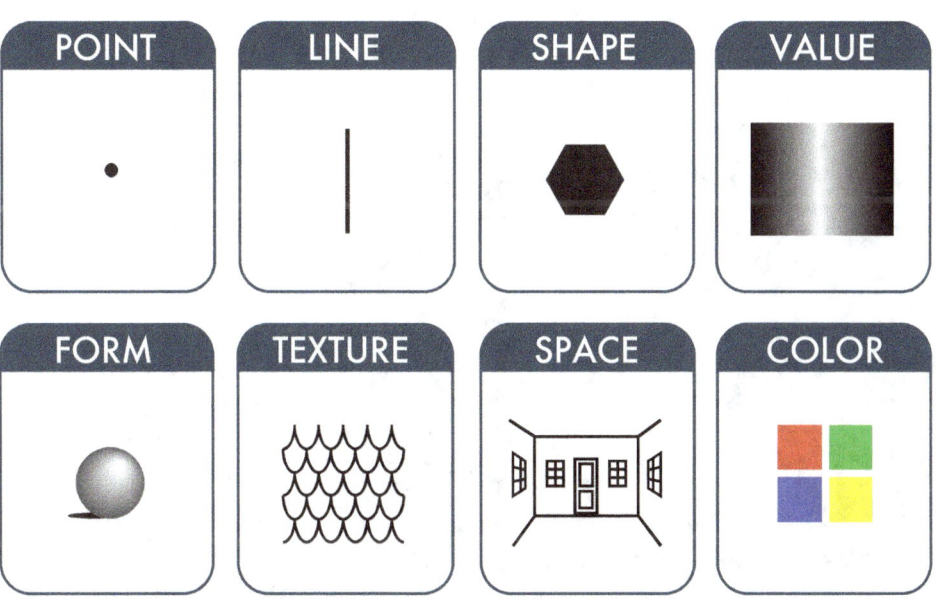

When we add intersecting lines or value to that shape, we can create the powerful illusion of depth on a two-dimensional surface, also known as form and space. Just like a child's basic building blocks which can be arranged in an infinite number of combinations, the elements are the most fundamental components used in the construction of an infinite number of images.

THE ELEMENTS: POINT

POINT

LINE

SHAPE

VALUE

FORM

TEXTURE

SPACE

COLOR

It may be tempting to think of a point as synonymous with a dot or very small circle but in fact a point is a much more ubiquitous component of visual compositions. A point may be indicative of a position in space and might be represented visually or might have no length and breadth at all. Points often indicate the beginning or end of a line or a point of convergence or divergence within a composition. Using a technique called pointillism, points can even be used to create value based on the varied density of their application.

Many of the other elements of art and design could not exist without points. A line requires at least two points; one at either end to indicate where the line begins and ends. A planar geometric shape has vertices or corner points where the faces of the shape converge and even a circle has a center point. Depictions of space often incorporate vanishing points where perspective lines converge in the distance.

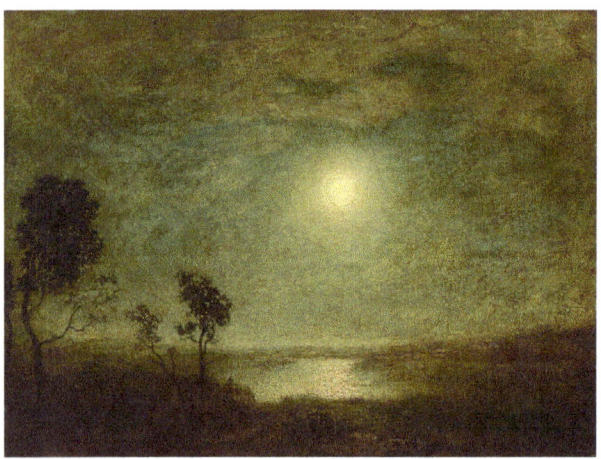

2. Ralph Albert Blake, *Moonlight*, 1886/1895

In Ralph Albert Blake's 1895 painting *Moonlight* [figure 2], it may seem that the only point is the bright moonlight at the center of the composition which radiates outward but we can also see that the body of water in the painting seems to converge at a bright point on the horizon, which is a perspective point called a vanishing point. The line of the horizon crosses the line of the distant tree trunk, forming an intersectional point. The viewer is also drawn to the point formed by the moonlight making it the focal point for the composition. As you can see, compositions can contain many different kinds of point.

KINDS OF POINT

Points are most often indicated by the beginning, end, convergence, or divergence of compositional components.

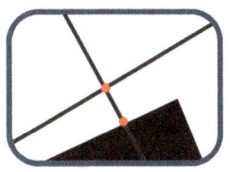

INTERSECTIONAL POINT
An intersectional point occurs when two lines or shapes meet. This kind of point will draw attention to the intersection.

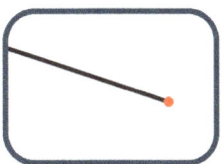

END OR TERMINAL POINT
An end or terminal point defines the place at which a line or a shape stops.

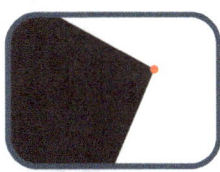

CORNER POINT OR VERTEX POINT
A corner or vertex point occurs at the juncture of two edges. An acute vertex feels sharp or fast and an obtuse vertex feels open or slow.

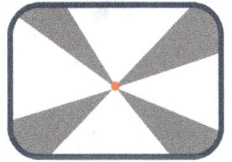

CONVERGENT POINT
Convergent points define the place at which shapes or lines come together. This can imply a deep space and create the sense of motion.

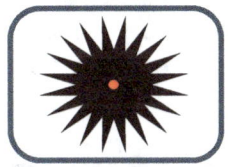

DIVERGENT POINT
Divergent points occur when elements in a composition radiate from a central place. This can create a sense of outward motion.

IMPLIED POINT
An implied point occurs when the eye follows a line to a point of convergence even if the line has ended. This can activate an empty space.

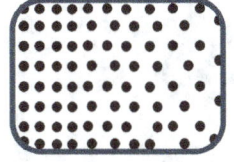

VALUE POINT
Points can create value and texture based on proximity, often called stippling or pointillism. The closer the points, the darker the value.

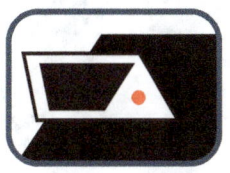

FOCAL POINT
A focal point is where the eye gravitates toward in a composition. This can be the result of emphasis, isolation, convergence, or contrast.

3

POINT VARIATIONS

In addition to points that are represented visually in a composition, some points are part of systems or concepts.

PERSPECTIVE VANISHING POINTS

Perspective is a complex visual system that allows the artist or designer to create an accurate visual representation of three-dimensional space on a two-dimensional plane. The system

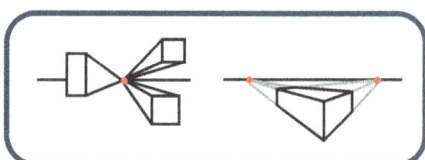

relies heavily on vanishing points, or the points at which perspective lines converge. These systems often use one or two vanishing points, though complex scenarios can contain many.

BALANCING POINTS

Balancing points in a composition may refer to internal elements within the composition or the composition as a whole. We will look at balance in depth as a principle but for the purpose of

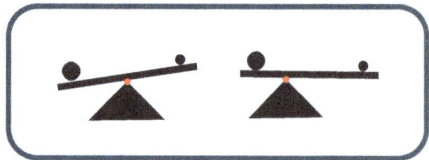

discussing point, a balancing point is the apex of the fulcrum where the elements being balanced pivot. An unbalanced composition will result in more or visually heavier elements on one side of the balancing point and a balanced composition will have equal visual weight on both sides of the balancing point.

In Edouard Vuillard's *Four Ladies with Fancy Hats* [figure 3], we can see the use of points to create texture and value. The points become less dense toward the top of the composition resulting in a lighter value.

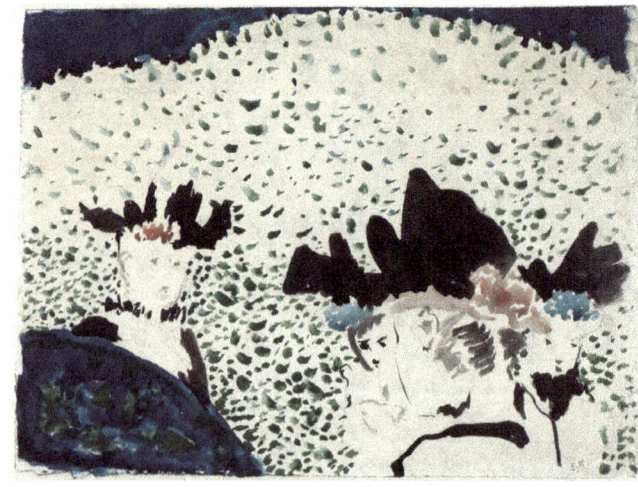

3. Edouard Vuillard, *Four Ladies with Fancy Hats*, 1892/93

Points can make or break a visual composition. For example, emphasizing a strong focal point within the composition can capture a viewer's attention while a misunderstanding of vanishing points can result in an unintentionally confusing depiction of three-dimensional space.

As visual observers, we are drawn to points in our environment, whether a pinpoint of light in the dark or the point where the hand of a clock intersects the circle of numbers on its face. Points serve to lead the viewer's eye around the composition as they involuntarily focus on beginnings and endings, and moments of convergence or intersection.

APPLYING COMPOSITION PRINCIPLES TO POINTS

As with all of the elements of art and design, points can be strategically arranged in order to create a particular effect, from a harmonious sense of unity to the chaos implied by excessive variety.

BALANCE

PROPORTION

CONTRAST

REPETITION

RHYTHM

PATTERN

MOVEMENT

EMPHASIS

UNITY

VARIETY

THE ELEMENTS: LINE

POINT
LINE
SHAPE
VALUE
FORM
TEXTURE
SPACE
COLOR

The element of line is one of the most familiar in the study of art and design and is often associated with drawing. We easily recognize the act of pulling a pencil across paper as the making of a line but it is also true that the pencil itself is a line and less obviously, that simply pointing the pencil in the direction of the paper implies an invisible line.

We can see implied line used to direct the viewer's attention in Leonardo da Vinci's 15th century mural *The Last Supper* [figure 4]. The apostles' gestures and gazes move the audience through the composition, leading us to Christ at the center of the composition. Perspective lines also converge to a single vanishing point just behind Christ's head. The exception is Thomas whose upward pointed index finger indicates heavenly ascent.

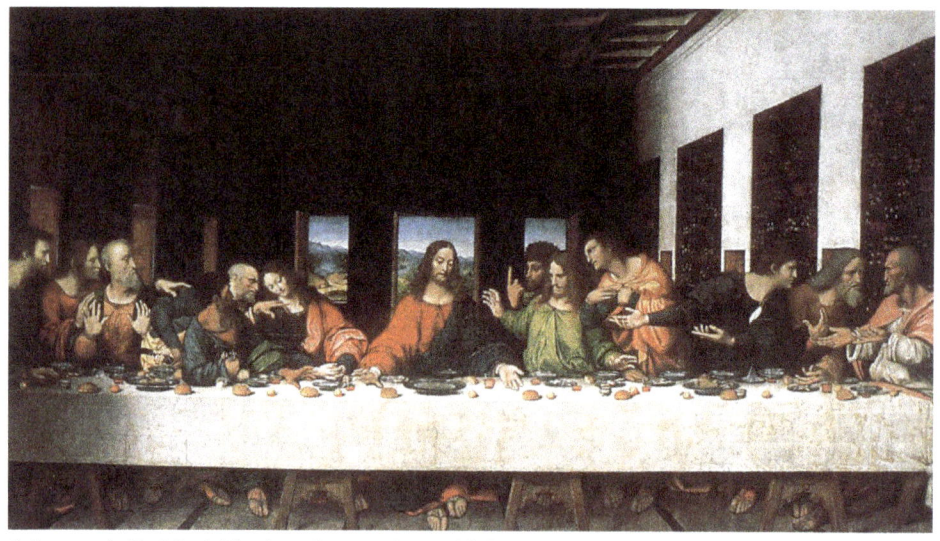

4. Leonardo Da Vinci, *The Last Supper*, Late 15th Century

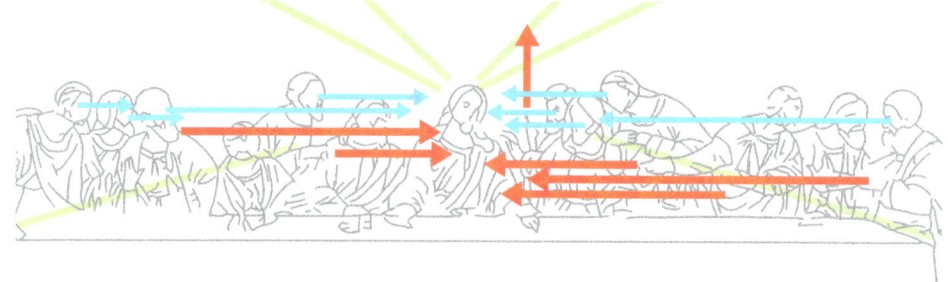

KINDS OF LINE

Line is widely variable in terms of direction, thickness, and visibility.

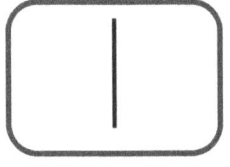

VERTICAL LINE
A vertical line can feel strong and forceful. It can imply a tree or human form in a natural setting or a tall building in an urban environment.

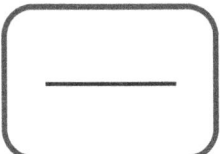

HORIZONTAL LINE
A horizontal line feels sedentary and grounding. It is most often associated with the horizon or the calm surface of a body of water.

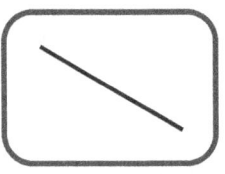

DIAGONAL LINE
Diagonal lines are dynamic and exciting. They create an illusion of movement and dimension and a feeling of sliding from top to bottom.

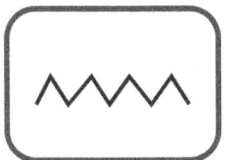

ZIGZAG OR JAGGED LINE
Zigzag or jagged lines change direction abruptly and feel agitated, fast, or uninviting. They would feel unpleasant to touch.

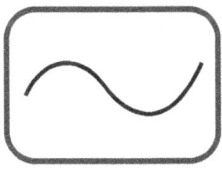

CURVED LINE
Curved lines are smooth and inviting. They often move through space slowly and would feel pleasant to touch.

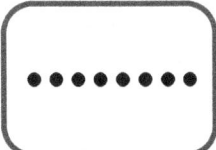

IMPLIED LINE
Implied lines are lines that are completed by our mind as we follow them. They engage our senses in the active creation of the line.

DELINEATING LINE
A delineating line is the boundary between shapes. These lines are created at the edges of where one shape ends and another begins.

CALLIGRAPHIC LINE
Calligraphic lines change width as they move through space creating visual interest. They are often associated with hand-made marks.

LINE VARIATIONS

Changes to line can greatly impact our perception of its meaning or implication. Our feelings about lines are closely tied to our experience of physical phenomenon. For example, a smooth line may feel slow and easy, even comforting, versus a jagged line which will feel more agitated and unpleasant. A wobbly line or a line that frequently doubles back on itself may feel unsure. A thick line can feel sturdy but also clunky or awkward and a thin line may feel precise but can also feel noncommittal.

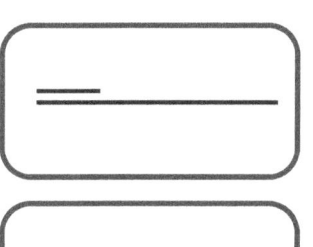

LENGTH
A long line can feel slow and indicate a horizon or division whereas a short line will tend to feel abrupt.

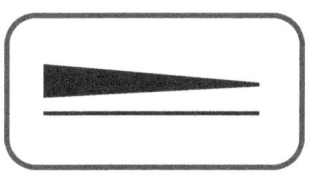

WIDTH
Lines that vary in width feel sensitive and careful. Thick lines can feel heavy or sturdy and thin lines can feel light or agile.

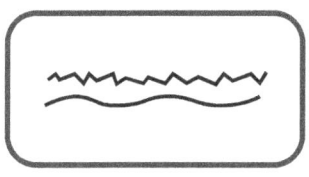

TEXTURE
Similar to physical touch, a smooth line will feel comfortable and a jagged line will feel unpleasant or agitated.

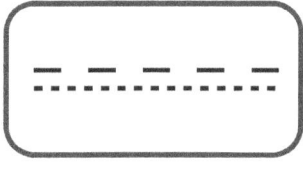

CONTINUITY
Implied lines often have varying degrees of continuity. The closer the pieces of a line, the more easily they read as line.

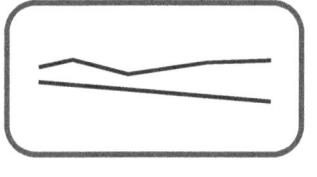

DIRECTIONALITY
A change in direction will give the line additional complexity and interrupt or slow the speed of the line.

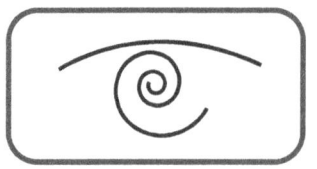

CURVE DEGREE
The tighter the curve of a line, the more intensity the line will have like the winding of a spring.

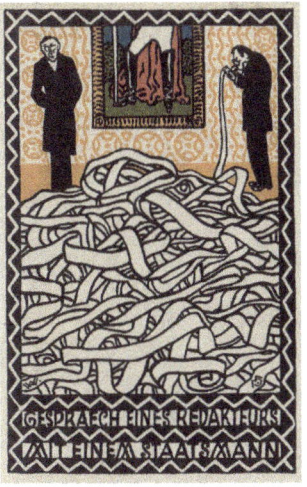

In Moriz Jung's illustration *The Editor's Conversation with the Statesman* [figure 5], the long, convoluted line of the scrolling paper is used to portray the absurdity of a politician's long-winded speech-writing. The lines overlap with such complexity that it is impossible to follow it from beginning to end, leaving the poor editor with an equally impossible task.

Line can be used to not only delineate an item from its surroundings like a coloring book; it is also a powerful tool capable of translating a feeling to the viewer.

5. Moriz Jung, *Gespräch eines Redakheurs mit einem Staatsmann*, 1907

APPLYING COMPOSITION PRINCIPLES TO LINE

Line is a versatile building block of composition and necessary to form the boundaries of shapes. When combined with principles of art and design, it has the power to communicate an abundance of information.

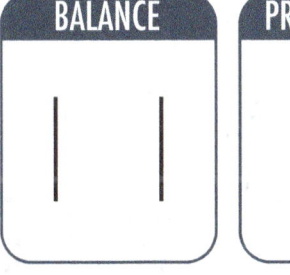

BALANCE

PROPORTIO N

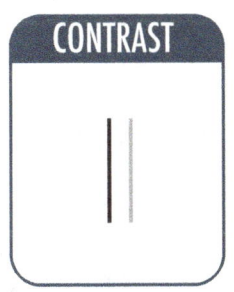

CONTRAST

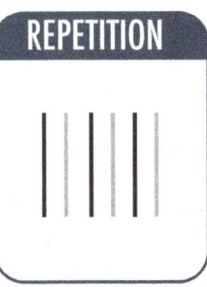

REPETITION

RHYTHM

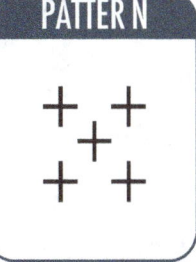

PATTER N

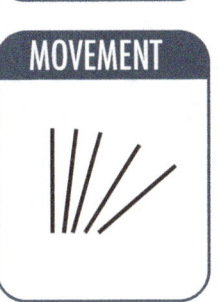

MOVEMENT

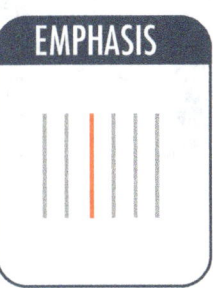

EMPHASIS

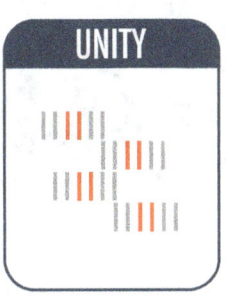

UNITY

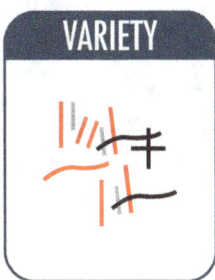

VARIETY

9

THE ELEMENTS: SHAPE

POINT

LINE

SHAPE

VALUE

FORM

TEXTURE

SPACE

COLOR

The first truly two-dimensional element in our list is shape. While point and line may have only one dimension a shape must have both height and width. We may associate line with the act of drawing but in even the most rudimentary drawing the lines most often form shapes. We navigate the world largely by recognizing the edges or boundaries between objects which brings shape into the realm of the tangible, connecting it strongly to our sense of physicality and touch.

In Felix Vallotton's 1898 woodcut print, *Le Gagnant (The Winner)* [figure 6] the artist depicts the exciting final moment of a horse race using only shapes without any variation in value. The viewer is drawn to the figure in white whose verticality reflects the vertical shapes in the fence below. Arms stretching down diagonally to cross the strong verticals of the fence add to the feeling of movement. In the background, soft clouds stand in contrast to the chaotic scene below.

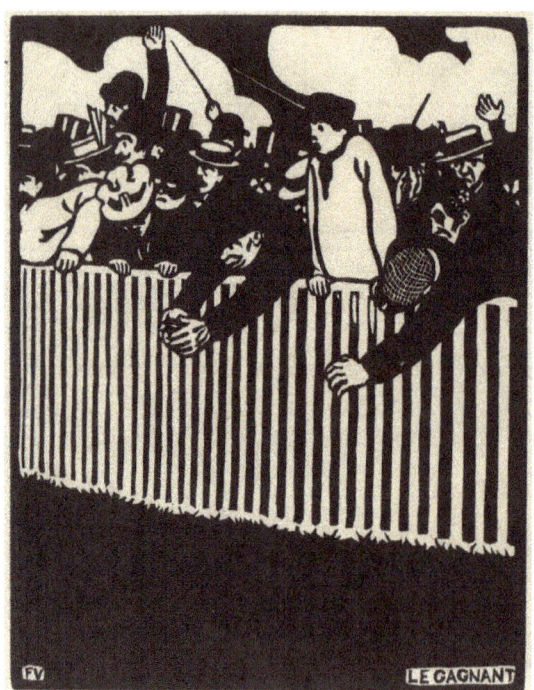

6. Félix Vallotton, *Le Gagnant*, 1898

We imagine the physical feeling of shapes. Though we cannot touch clouds, we describe them as soft. We sense the rhythmic sound that the fence might make if we were to brush our hand across it as we walked by. The shapes of hats and faces and arms crushing together with great complexity creates a feeling of chaos and density that would be physically difficult to navigate. The artist takes advantage of these physical associations to create a create a feeling in the viewer despite using minimal visual information.

KINDS OF SHAPE

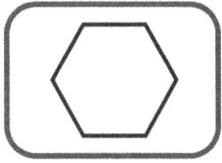

GEOMETRIC SHAPE
A geometric shape can indicate solidity but also rigidity. It indicates structure and is more associated with man-made objects than nature.

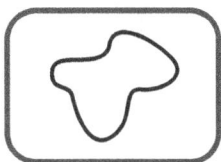

ORGANIC SHAPE
An organic shape is free-flowing and is may remind a viewer of forms that are found in natural environments.

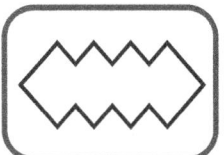

HARD EDGED SHAPE
Hard shapes are often geometric and feel unfriendly if one imagines touching them. These shapes can create a sense of structure.

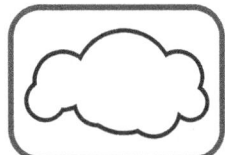

SOFT EDGED SHAPE
A soft shape is friendly and inviting. These shapes are often organic and reflect a tactile experience that is comforting.

IMPLIED SHAPE
Implied shapes are not directly bound by their edges but are instead indicated by their surroundings.

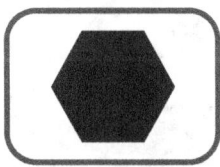

POSITIVE SHAPE
A positive shape is easily seen and is comforting to the viewer as a way to differentiate the figure and the ground against which it is seen.

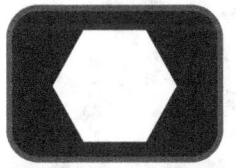

NEGATIVE SHAPE
A negative shape is defined by the ground that encloses or surrounds it and is often more disconcerting for the viewer.

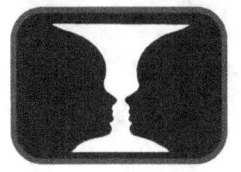

AMBIGUOUS SHAPE
Ambiguous shapes are the most visually disconcerting for the viewer because it is not clear whether the figure or ground is the shape.

ELEMENTS

SHAPE

SHAPE VARIATIONS

When we think of shapes, we often gravitate toward the simple geometries that we learn as children. However, shapes are widely variable and each has an individual character depending on a variety of factors.

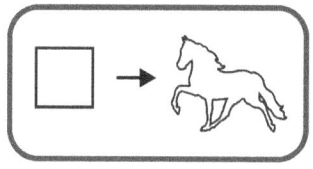

SIMPLICITY versus COMPLEXITY
Simple shapes are easily comprehensible and can feel clean and minimal. Complex shapes can be visually exciting.

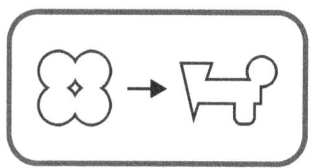

REGULARITY versus IRREGULARITY
Regular shapes are predictable and comfortable, even rhythmic. Irregular shapes can feel chaotic or whimsical.

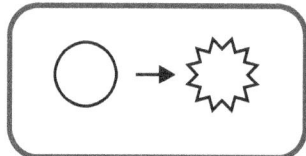

EDGE TEXTURE
Smooth edged shapes feel comfortable and welcoming whereas jagged edged shapes can feel rough or sharp.

Shape has the power to reduce an image to its most basic components or to create extraordinary complexity. In Alfred Stieglitz's photograph *Shadows in Lake* [figure 7], the figures are reduced to ghostly silhouettes superimposed on the textured water. The complexities and specificities of the object-matter that may have distracted the viewer from the composition are eliminated in favor of simple shapes.

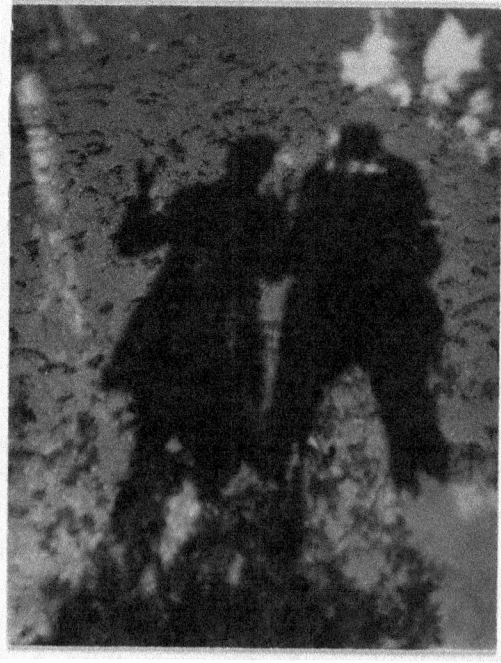

7. Alfred Stieglitz, *Shadows in Lake*, 1916

Complexity can be also be visually engaging. A silhouette of the complex girders of the Eiffel Tower captures our attention when placed next to the monolithic structure of the Empire State Building. The complexity of the intricately intertwined beams creates texture and dynamism whereas the solidity of the Empire State Building feels heavy and sullen.

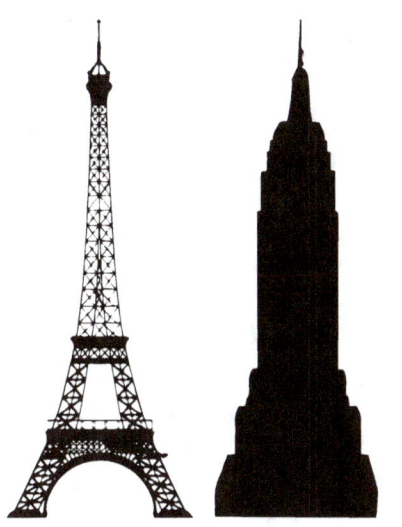

APPLYING COMPOSITION PRINCIPLES TO SHAPE

Organizing shapes into particular configurations has the potential to expand on the variations within individual shapes. For example, a repeated pattern of jagged shapes will emphasize the sense of texture beyond the single shape.

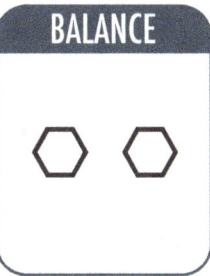

BALANCE

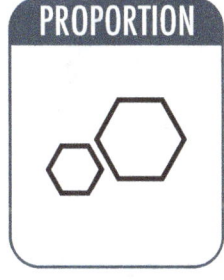

PROPORTION

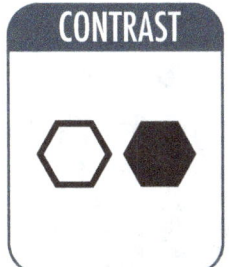

CONTRAST

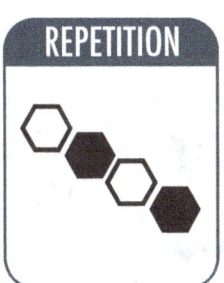

REPETITION

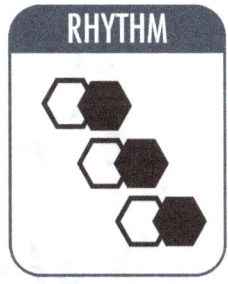

RHYTHM

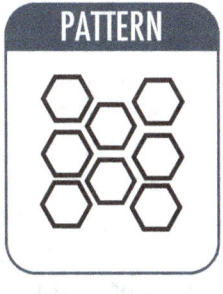

PATTERN

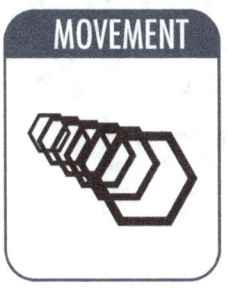

MOVEMENT

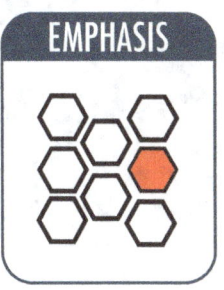

EMPHASIS

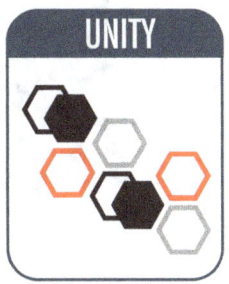

UNITY

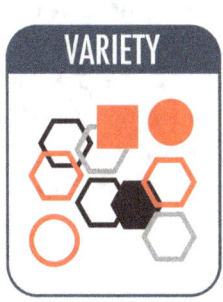

VARIETY

THE ELEMENTS: VALUE

POINT
LINE
SHAPE
VALUE
FORM
TEXTURE
SPACE
COLOR

We rely on reflected light to differentiate objects from their surroundings and to comprehend their dimension and the nature of their surface. Amazingly, our ability to observe subtle variations in value allows us to comprehend even minute differences in the texture of objects without ever touching them.

Value, or the difference between the lightness or darkness of a surface, is determined by how much light is reflected back to our eyes. A white object reflects about 90% of the light whereas a black object only reflects about 3%. This inability to see in the absence of light is why we are often afraid of the dark and why horror movies deploy dark or low-key value to create a sense of dread.

Joseph De Martini's *Seascape* [figure 8] uses middle key, low-contrast value to create a moody scene with moonlight illuminating the surrounding clouds and reflecting brightly off of the shoreline. Though he often worked in color, De Martini utilized only black and white paint in this composition to mimic the experience of seeing a scene in low light. In the absence of adequate light, photo-receptors called rods which do not help with color perception are primarily used for vision resulting in a reduced ability to see color at night.

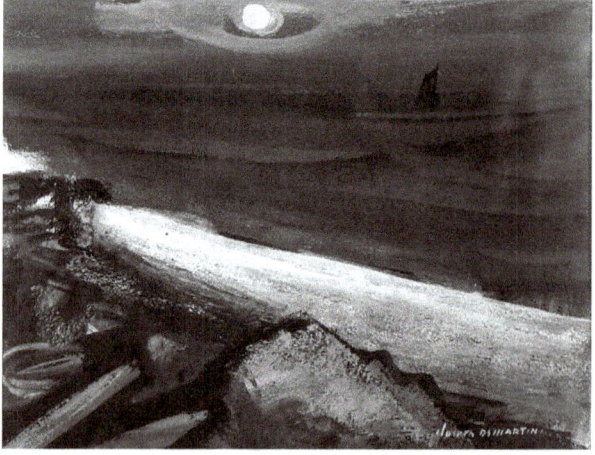

8. Joseph De Martini, *Seascape*, ca. 1938–39

14

KINDS OF VALUE

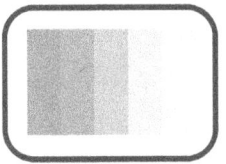

HIGH KEY VALUE
High key value incorporates lighter tones, is associated with positive feelings, and can give the impression of lightness or weightlessness.

LOW KEY VALUE
Low key value incorporates darker tones and feels heavy and dense. It is often associated with negative feelings such as fear or depression.

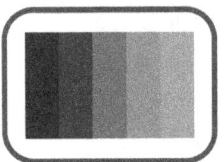

MIDDLE KEY VALUE
Middle key value is incorporates tones that are neither dark nor light. It can feel ambiguous or confusing like fog or dusk.

HIGH CONTRAST VALUE
High contrast value juxtaposes tones from opposing ends of the spectrum and is often attention grabbing and visual exciting.

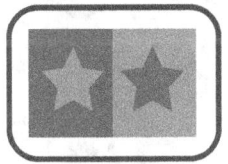

LOW CONTRAST VALUE
Low contrast or analogous value uses tones that are close to one another and can feel either calm or ambiguous.

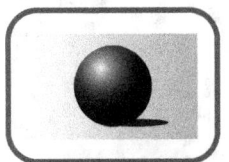

CHIAROSCURO
Chiaroscuro (from the Italian meaning light and dark) is a technique that creates drama by using strong lights and darks that model form.

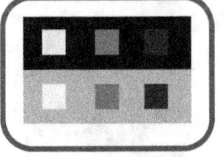

RELATIVE VALUE
Relative value is a phenomenon that makes values appear lighter or darker in relation to the surrounding tones.

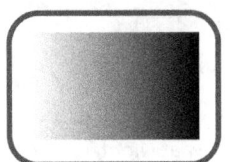

GRADIENT VALUE
Gradient value is a smooth transition from one value to the next and is often used to describe dimensional forms.

VALUE VARIATIONS

While value may seem as simple as shades of gray, the ways in which we create and perceive value can vary dramatically, from pointillism to local value.

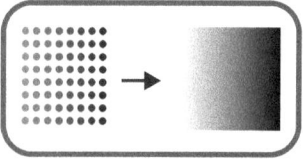

VALUE CONTINUITY
We often think of value shifts happening smoothly but in cases such as a reflective surface value makes larger jumps.

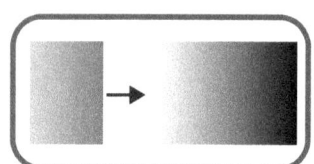

NARROW versus FULL RANGE VALUE
A narrow range of value may be mostly dark, mostly light, or mostly gray. A full range is everything between white and black.

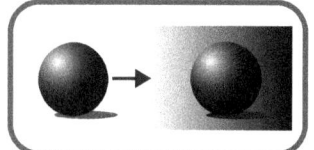

LOCAL versus GLOBAL VALUE
Local value describes the value of an object or element within a composition. Global value describes the overall composition.

Artists, especially those working in photographic media, are fascinated by visual phenomenon involving light. In Anne Goldwaite's painting *A Window at Night* [figure 9] the artist explores the unusual depiction of a window as the dark backdrop for an object rather than a source of light. To emphasize the sense of night vision she uses only black and white paint. Unlike De Martini's *Seascape* [figure 8] this piece uses a full range of value to create a crisp depiction of a well lit plant. Despite being on a shallow windowsill the full range of value creates the illusion of a dimensional form.

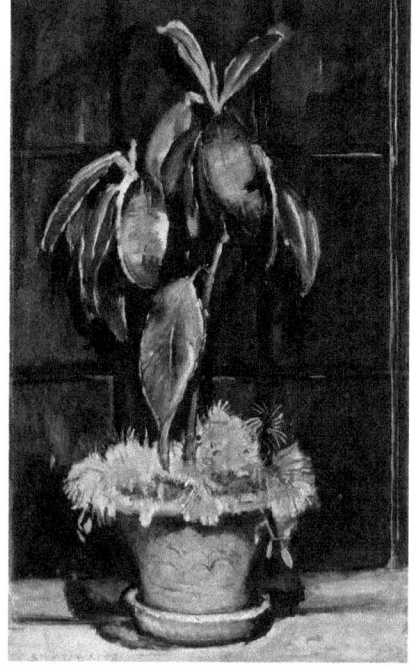

9. Anne Goldthwaite,
A Window at Night, ca. 1933

We also associate value with negative or positive feelings. For example, horror movie posters are often predominately low-key value while comedy posters are often high-key value. A mystery movie poster may utilize middle-key value to create a sense of ambiguity.

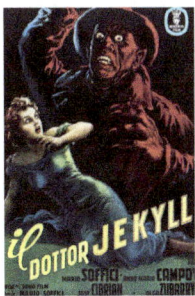
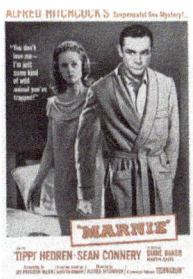
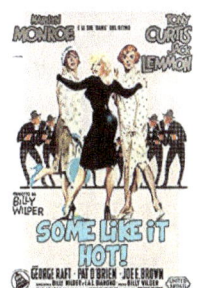

APPLYING COMPOSITION PRINCIPLES TO VALUE

The compositional arrangement of value can dramatically change its impact on the viewer. Balancing value is especially important as dark elements are perceived as much heavier than light elements.

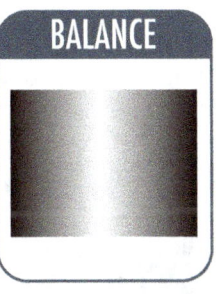
BALANCE

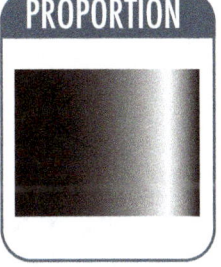
PROPORTION

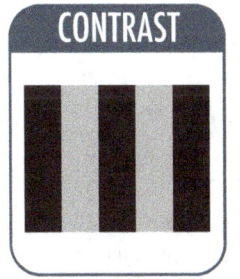
CONTRAST

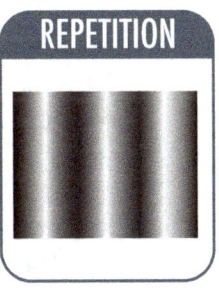
REPETITION

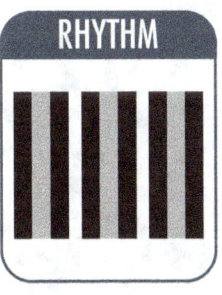
RHYTHM

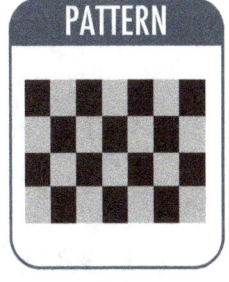
PATTERN

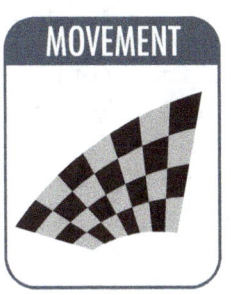
MOVEMENT

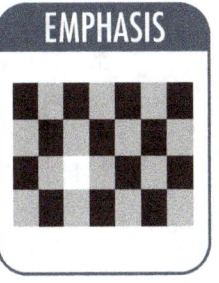
EMPHASIS

UNITY

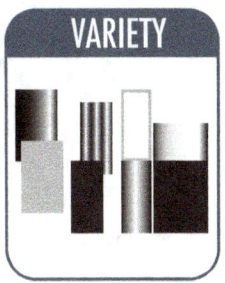
VARIETY

17

THE ELEMENTS: FORM

POINT
LINE
SHAPE
VALUE
► FORM
TEXTURE
SPACE
COLOR

The perception of dimensionality using changes in value, even when the image exists only on a two-dimensional plane, is known as form. We utilize our ability to perceive form constantly in our daily lives, from simple operations like holding this book in your hands to complex scenarios like performing surgery. The illusion of form on a two-dimensional surface can also range dramatically in complexity, from the simplest illustration of a cube to incredibly complex 3D animated films.

While form can be created using point (pointillism) or line (overlap and intersection), it is most often associated with the element of value. We navigate the spatial complexities of the world utilizing visual perception. This allows artists and designers to create illusory images that trick the mind using the hallmarks of dimensional perception on a two-dimensional surface. While this is sometimes done with traditional techniques like drawing, painting, and photography, we perpetually find new ways to perform these illusions using technologies like virtual reality and computer animation.

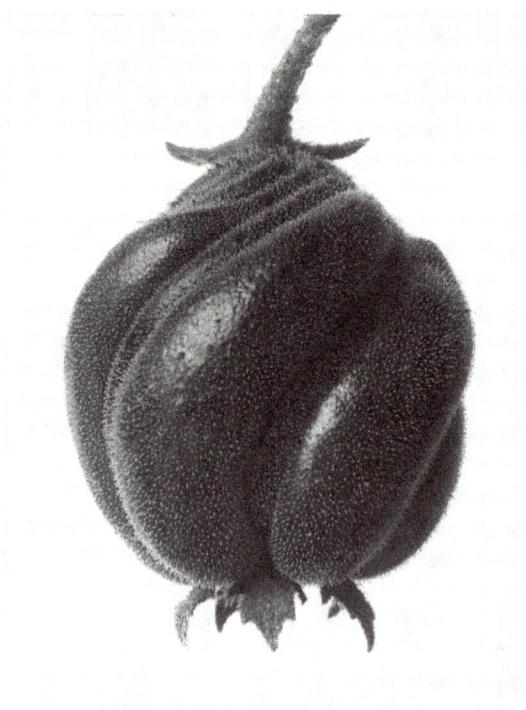

As with line and shape, form readily connects to our non-visual senses. For example, a smooth form appears to be pleasant to touch while a jagged form recalls a less comfortable experience. Form can be a powerful way to invoke the viewer's tactile memory and mirror our experience of the physical world despite the limitations of two-dimensional images.

10. Karl Blossfeldt, *Blumenbachia hieronymi*, 1915-25

KINDS OF FORM

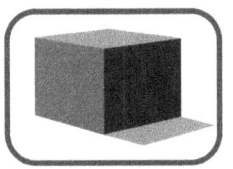

GEOMETRIC FORMS
Geometric forms are constructed using points, lines, and angles to create the illusion of depth. They can feel unnatural or man-made, and predictable.

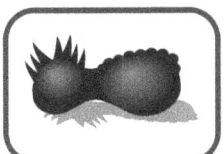

ORGANIC FORMS
Organic forms use curves and smooth gradations to create the illusion of depth and can feel natural, unpredictable, and free-flowing.

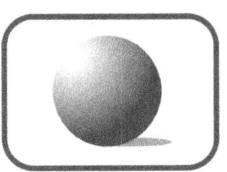

POSITIVE FORMS
Positive forms are defined by the illusion of surface created by value and edge. They feel tangible, physical, and solid.

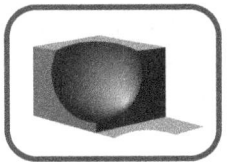

NEGATIVE OR IMPLIED FORMS
Negative forms are defined by the surface of surrounding forms. These forms feel like an empty space and can connote absence.

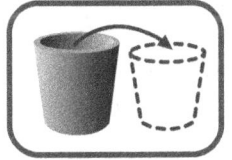

VOLUMETRIC FORMS
Volumetric forms create the illusion of an interior space or structure and emphasize the volume of an object rather than its surface or mass.

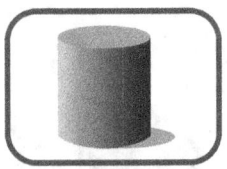

SOLID FORMS
Solid forms emphasize the surface but also imply density of mass. They feel heavier and more concrete than volumetric objects.

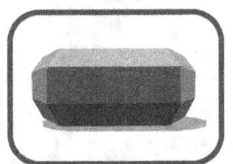

PLANAR FORMS
Planar objects create the illusion of form using individual flat plans to describe the surface. Planar objects feel mechanical and man-made.

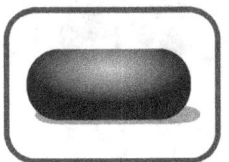

CURVILINEAR FORMS
Curvilinear forms utilize gradations of value to describe smooth surfaces that feel friendly and comfortable to touch.

FORM VARIATIONS

Form can invoke dramatically different recollections of the physical world for the viewer whether calling to mind the familiar and comfortable or the dramatic and unstable. By mirroring physical experiences form forces the viewer to inhabit the picture.

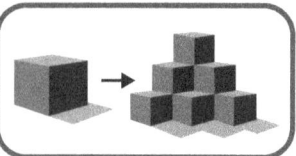

SIMPLE versus COMPLEX OR COMPOUND
Simple forms are easily comprehended and feel clean and crisp while complex forms can feel ornate or challenging.

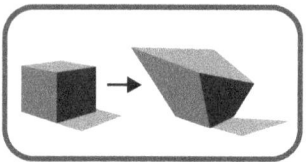

SYMMETRICAL versus ASYMMETRICAL
While symmetry is predictable and sometimes comforting, asymmetry has the potential to add dynamism and movement to a form.

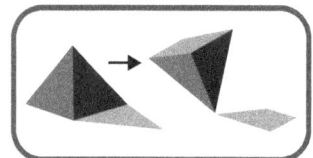

STABLE versus UNSTABLE
We recognize form stability and instability in our bodies. Simply standing on one leg versus two illustrates our empathic experience of stability.

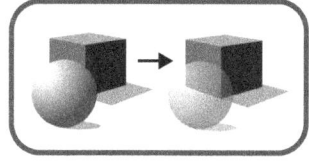

OPAQUE versus TRANSPARENT
While we often think of forms as solids, they can also have varying degrees of opacity creating the perception of differences in density.

Giorgio Sommer's 1873 photograph of a plaster cast of one of the victims of the volcanic eruption at Pompeii [figure 11] emphasizes form in order to instill in the viewer a sense of physical empathy. The figure appears in a pose that recalls

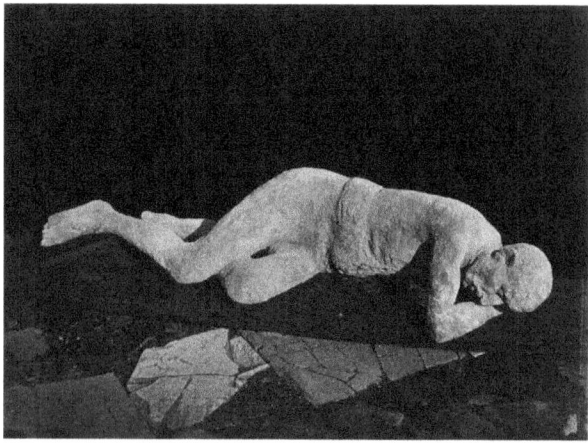

11. Giorgio Sommer, *Impronte umane*, 1873

a silent and peaceful sleep. The image uses relative value to highlight the white plaster which stands in sharp contrast to the black background, emphasizing the subtle changes in value that give the figure a recognzable roundness. The black background which hangs heavily above the figure lke a starless night as well as the form's familiarity beckons us to imagine the deep and unending silence of his sleep.

Form has the power to captivate our imagination through mimicry, to create in our minds experiences that we may never have had, and ultimately to use the hallmarks of the physical world to create illusions that the viewer cannot help but enter into.

APPLYING COMPOSITION PRINCIPLES TO FORM

As with previous elements, form can be arranged in a variety of ways to create different effects and because form mirrors the physical world, we readily recognize arrangements that utilize physical phenomenon.

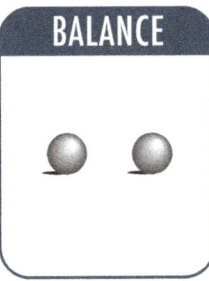

BALANCE

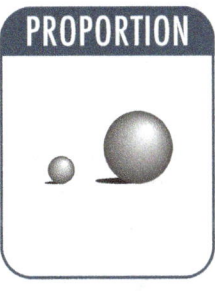

PROPORTION

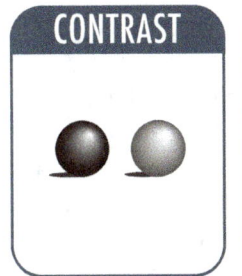

CONTRAST

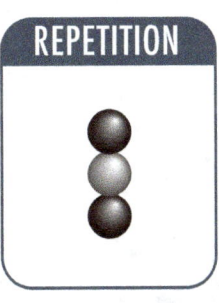

REPETITION

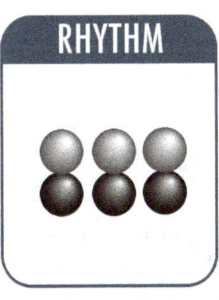

RHYTHM

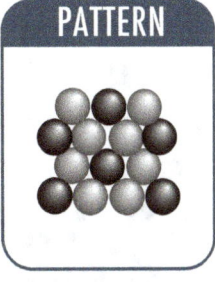

PATTERN

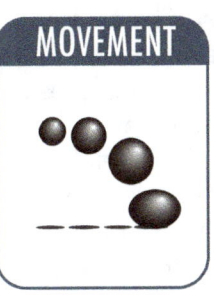

MOVEMENT

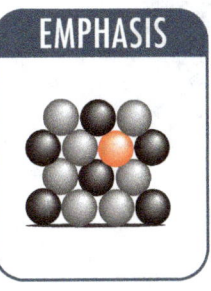

EMPHASIS

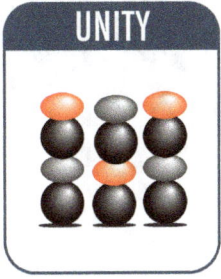

UNITY

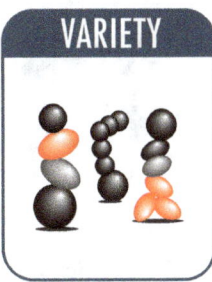

VARIETY

THE ELEMENTS: TEXTURE

POINT
LINE
SHAPE
VALUE
FORM
▶ TEXTURE
SPACE
COLOR

The art element that is perhaps most related to our sense of physical touch is texture. We experience visual texture primarily through repeating differences in value and these changes can range from gradual to rapid and subtle to dramatic. As darker values create the illusion of receding and lighter values create the illusion of advancing toward the viewer, these changes recall the experience of touching a surface with rapid and repeating changes in physical depth.

Artists and designers also utilize texture beyond the realm of illusions by incorporating techniques like collage's layers of paper and impasto painting's thick applications of paint. These physical techniques not only add visual interest but also reveal aspects of the creative process to the viewer.

In Torsten Renqvist's 1964 etching *The Edge of the Forest* [figure 12], dense overlapping lines mimic the interwoven branches of a forbidding thicket. The chaotic texture mirrors the physical feeling of a tangled forest and prevents the viewer from accessing an easy path through the composition. The viewer not only sees these lines but imagines the discomforting tactile experience of physically encountering the tangled undergrowth.

Despite its potential to repel the viewer with complexity, texture can also serve to engage by creating visual interest. Tightly repetitive textures can be intricate and soft while bold textures can lead us through a composition like stepping stones.

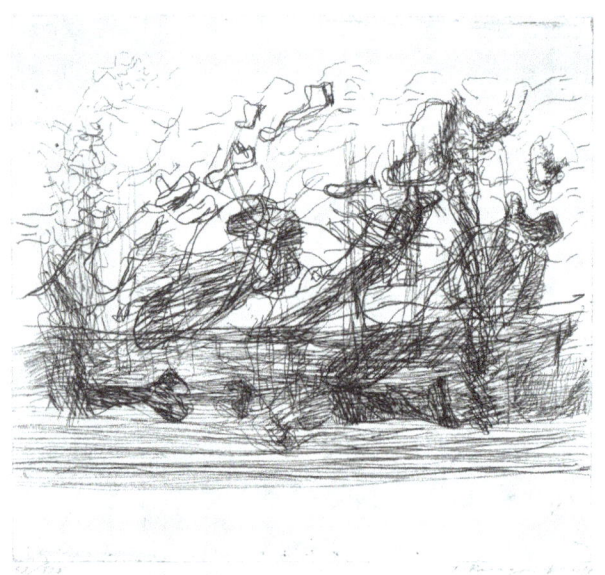

12. Torsten Renqvist, *The edge of the forest*, 1964

KINDS OF TEXTURE

Texture can be physical like collage or strictly visual like patterned wallpaper. Visual textures can be as widely varied as our physical experience of touch. We can even mimic textures from our environment in order to call to mind prior touch-based experiences.

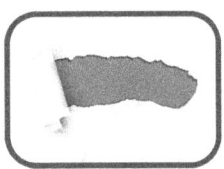

PHYSICAL TEXTURE
Physical or tactile texture is a change in surface that can be touched, like collaged paper, thick paint strokes, or even smooth paper.

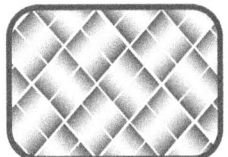

VISUAL OR IMPLIED TEXTURE
Visual or implied texture uses variations in value to imply a change in surface. This can create visual interest by indicating touchability.

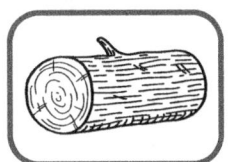

REPRESENTATIONAL TEXTURE
Representational texture uses the viewer's familiarity with the physical world to create the illusion of a known surface.

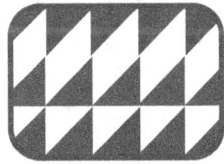

GEOMETRIC TEXTURE
Geometric texture uses line and shape to create tactility in an image. Geometric textures tend to feel unfriendly, hard, and precise.

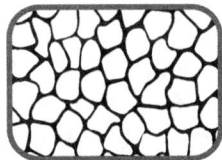

ORGANIC TEXTURE
Organic textures use irregular shapes and lines to create a varied surface that feels unpredictable and natural.

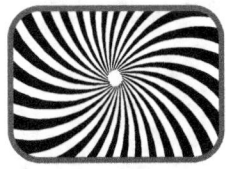

REGULAR TEXTURE
Regular textures use repeated shapes to create a strong sense of predictability and uniformity through pattern.

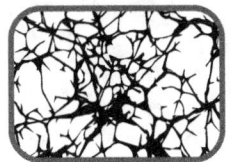

IRREGULAR TEXTURE
Irregular textures are often organic and feel unpredictable. The more irregular a texture is, the more chaotic it can feel.

TEXTURE VARIATIONS

As with physical texture, we can vary the viewer's experience by varying the visual textures within an image.

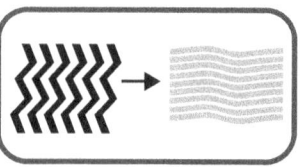

ROUGH versus SMOOTH TEXTURE
A rough texture can give the impression of an excited or agitated surface whereas a smooth texture can be soothing.

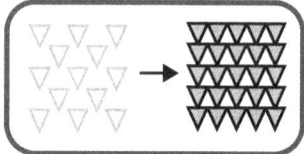

SPARSE versus DENSE TEXTURE
Textures can range from feeling almost solid to being very sparse. Density can create a feeling of impenetrability.

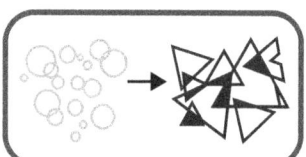

SOFT versus HARD TEXTURE
Soft textures feel more open and accessible and hard textures feel more forbidding and less friendly.

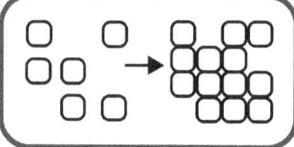

TEXTURAL CONTINUITY
A texture may be sparse but still consistent which is reassuring to the viewer. A texture that does not have continuity feels unpredictable.

Unlike the forbiddingly dense texture in Torsten Renqvist's landscape etching [figure 12], He Weipu's landscape [figure 13] features lush textures that invite the viewer to enter the composition. The smooth, organic marks create a soft texture that feels comforting despite the mountainous terrain and the foliage features rounded leaves that cradle the remote mountain shelter.

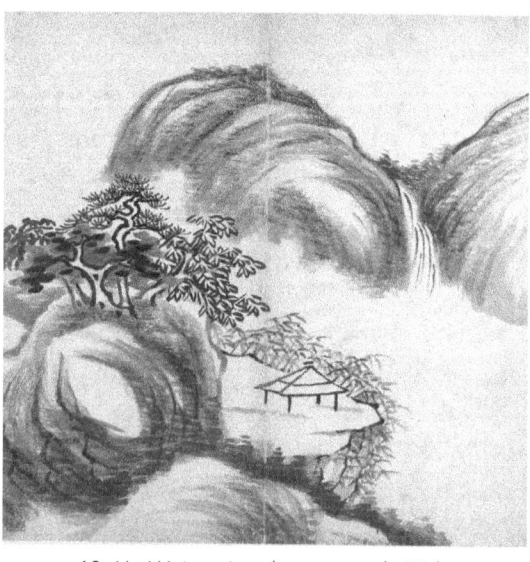

13. He Weipu, *Landscapes*, early 20th century

While both compositions portray landscape and prominently feature texture, they deploy this versatile element in very different ways in order to achieve starkly differing effects. In both cases we can see that texture adds to the visual interest of the composition by engaging our association with tactile experience, inviting the viewer to look more closely. However, in the prior image texture's versatility also has the power to repel by reminding the viewer of prior physically unpleasant experiences.

It is this versatility that makes texture a frequently utilized element in images that aim to conjure mood. Texture's ability to mirror our tactile experience gives it the power to engage our memory of the physical world.

APPLYING COMPOSITION PRINCIPLES TO TEXTURE

Texture can be arranged in ways that are as varied as our experience of the tactile world. These can create pleasant and inviting experiences, add visual interest, or be unpleasant and forbidding.

BALANCE

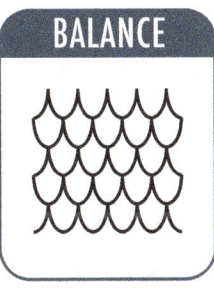

PROPORTION

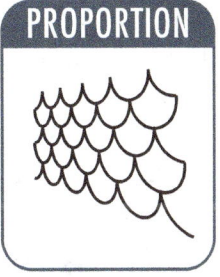

CONTRAST

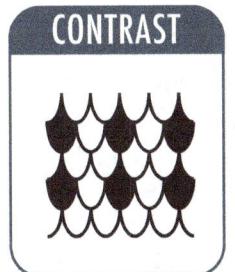

REPETITION

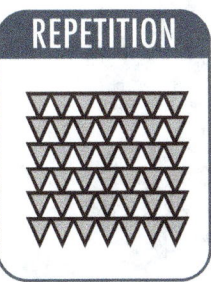

RHYTHM

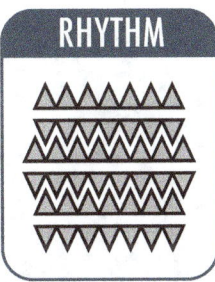

PATTERN

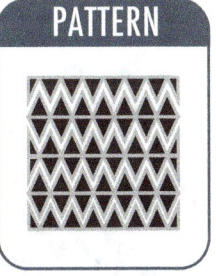

MOVEMENT

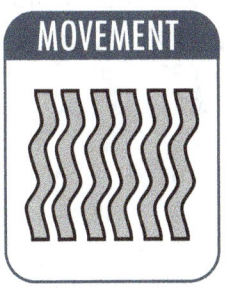

EMPHASIS

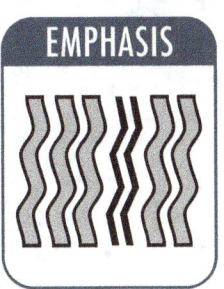

UNITY

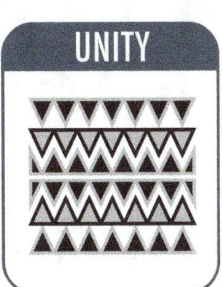

VARIETY

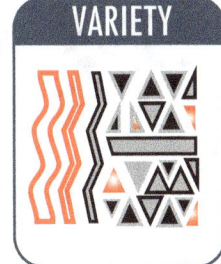

THE ELEMENTS: SPACE

POINT

LINE

SHAPE

VALUE

FORM

TEXTURE

SPACE

COLOR

Human eyes are positioned quite close together compared to many mammals, a feature which helps us to perceive depth with incredible accuracy. Our ancient ancestors gained success using this adaptation when hunting small game in complex environments. Even the earliest human attempts at translating the three-dimensional world onto a two-dimensional surface utilized spacial illusions that reflect our shared perception of depth. In the cave paintings of Lascaux, France, which are estimated to be up to 20,000 years old, animals appear to overlap one another or diminish in size as distances increase, creating the illusion of dimensional space.

While simply overlapping two components of a composition creates the sense that one is in front of the other, artists and designers often use complex systems to mimic our experience of dimensional space. In Thomas Flavell's drawing *Atlantic and Pacific* [figure 14], the artist uses a two-point perspective system in which the diagonal edges of the building appear to converge at a distant point. Supporting this illusion of depth is the use

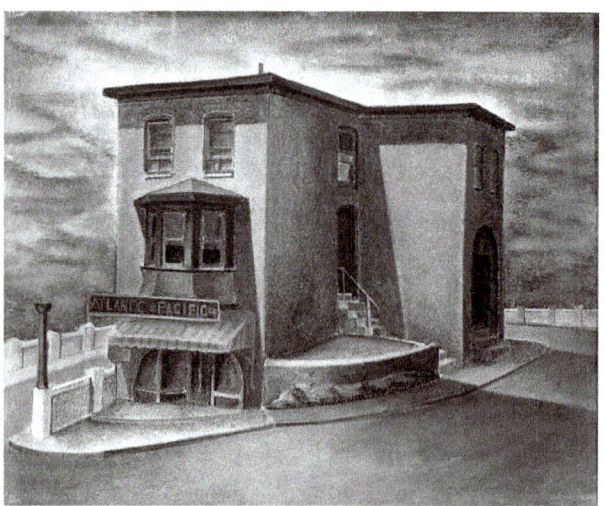

14. Thomas Flavell, *Atlantic and Pacific*, ca. 1940

of atmospheric perspective which gives distant objects less definition and contrast than those that are nearest to the viewer. The resulting image can trick the brain into an experience that is akin to looking out of a window at a scene rather than observing a representation on a two-dimensional surface.

Beyond the illusion of depth, images also contain spaces between components. These two-dimensional spaces are often referred to as positive and negative space. Positive space refers to the area of an image that we perceive as object and negative is the surrounding space.

KINDS OF SPACE

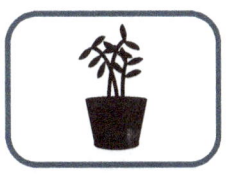
POSITIVE SPACE
Positive space is the area within a composition that is occupied by a primary object or design element and draws attention to that focal area.

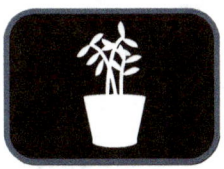
NEGATIVE SPACE
Negative space is the area between the primary element and the edge of the composition. Negative space defines positive shapes within.

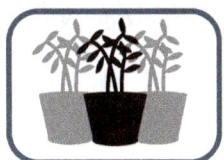
OVERLAPPING SPACE
Overlapping forms create the illusion of depth. The way in which a form or shape obscures other forms determines which object appears closer.

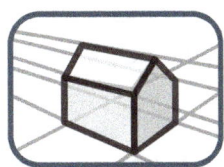
PERSPECTIVE SPACE
Perspective space uses vanishing points on a horizon line to create a consistent illusion of depth that mimics three-dimensional space.

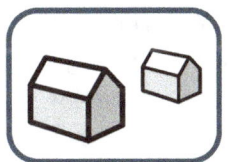
PROPORTIONAL SPACE
Proportional space uses the perceived change in scale that occurs as we get closer or further from an object.

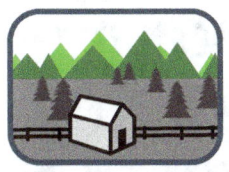
BACKGROUND SPACE
Background space is the plane furthest from the viewer and is often the least dominant part of the composition.

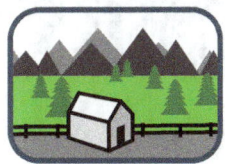
MIDDLE GROUND SPACE
Middle ground space is the plane between the background and foreground and serves to unify the planes and create consistency.

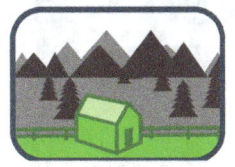
FOREGROUND SPACE
Foreground space is the plane closest to the viewer and is often the most dominant part of the composition with crisp edges and high contrast.

SPACE VARIATIONS

Whether portraying the vast open spaces of the American west or a shallow Roman frieze, variations in color and value can dramatically impact our perception of space.

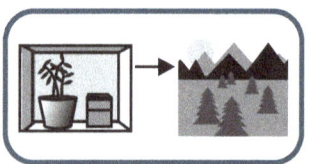

SHALLOW versus DEEP SPACE
A shallow space can feel constricted and forces a frontal view. A deep space allows the viewer to imagine traveling into the image.

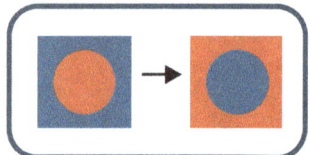

ADVANCING VS RECEDING COLOR
Warm colors appear to advance toward the viewer whereas cooler colors seem to recede into the distance.

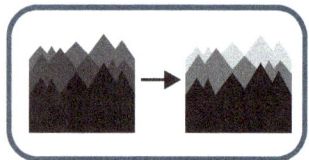

ATMOSPHERIC VALUE
As atmospheric particles accumulate over distance they obscure far-off objects, especially on hazy days.

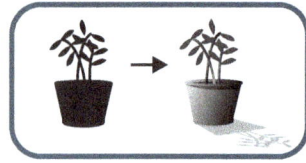

FLAT versus VOLUMETRIC SPACE
Flat space is two-dimensional and either positive (object) or negative (surrounding). Volumetric refers to three-dimensional space.

In addition to emphasizing depth by depicting the railing spindles as getting smaller and closer together as they become more distant, Félix Vallotton's illustration *The Moving Footway* [figure 15] uses of complex positive and negative space

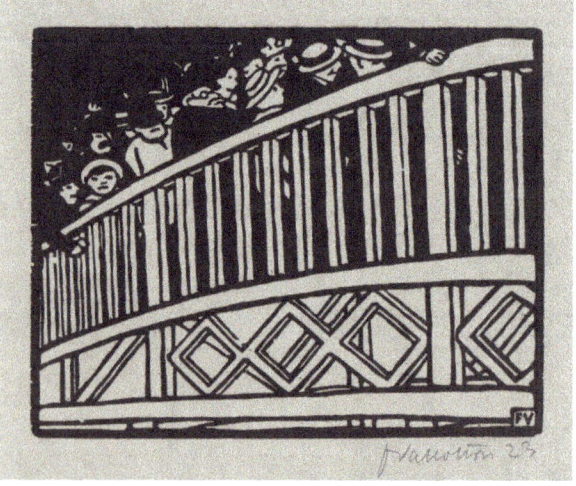

15. Félix Vallotton, *The Moving Footway, The World's Fair I*, 1901

relationships to create visual interest. The black area at the top left of the image serves as negative space and the light area at the bottom left depicting the underpinnings of the elevated walkway are positive space. The negative and positive space become interspersed and complex along the diagonal line formed by the crowd, portraying a feeling of chaotic movement and excitement.

Space not only reflects our navigation of the world using depth perception, it also allows the artist to create visually engaging compositions that capture our attention.

APPLYING COMPOSITION PRINCIPLES TO SPACE

Space can be modified to create dramatic effects using the principles of art and design because we subconsciously inhabit the spaces that we see, even when those spaces appear strictly as visual illusions.

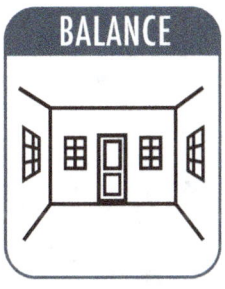
BALANCE

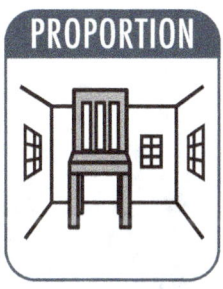
PROPORTION

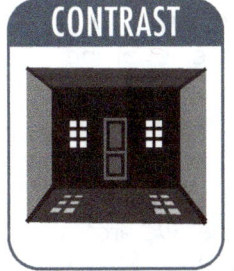
CONTRAST

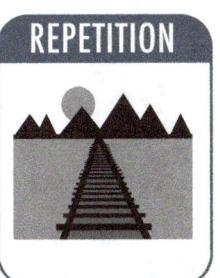
REPETITION

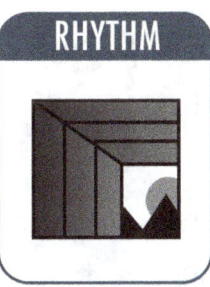
RHYTHM

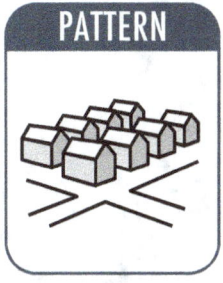
PATTERN

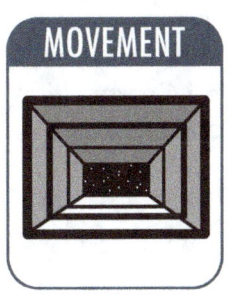
MOVEMENT

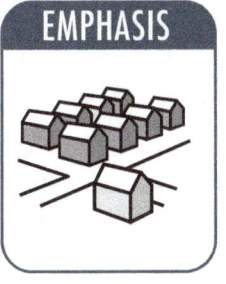
EMPHASIS

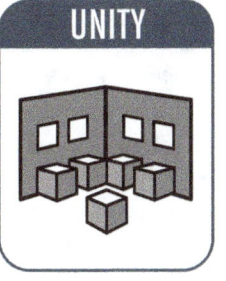
UNITY

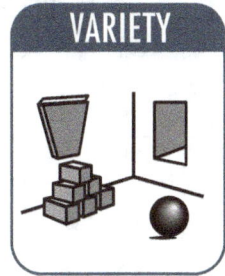
VARIETY

THE ELEMENTS: COLOR

POINT
LINE
SHAPE
VALUE
FORM
TEXTURE
SPACE
COLOR

Color is a deeply symbolic element and is often associated with mood and emotion. Warm colors evoke passion and speed while cool colors create a sense of calm or even sadness. We speak of "having the blues" when we are feeling down or we may "see red" when we are furious. Ambulances and stop signs use saturated red to catch our attention while hospital interiors frequently use tints of calming blue and green.

Color combinations add complexity and variety to our visual world. Professional sports teams create excitement by using complimentary colors in their uniforms which are on opposite sides of the color wheel and visually vibrate when placed next to one another. On the other hand, businesses that rely on customer trust use cool analogous colors to call to mind harmony.

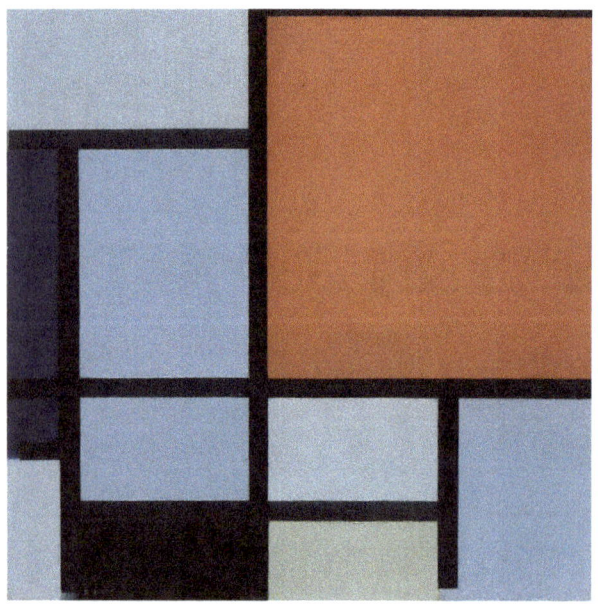

16. Piet Mondrian, *Composition*, 1921

In Piet Mondrian's *Composition* [figure 16], the artist is clearly calling our attention to the red square in the top right corner. Despite the intermingled complexity of the black lines and blue squares in left and bottom of the painting, it is the red that we are immediately drawn to. It is no mistake that this painting is entitled *Composition* as Mondrian was fascinated by the construction of images through the arrangement of their constituent components and the infinite number of variations that are possible despite the seemingly stringent limitation of the grid.

KINDS OF COLOR

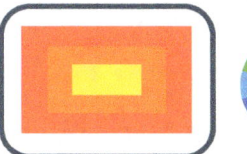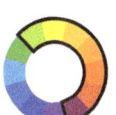

MONOCHROMATIC COLOR
Monochromatic color uses only tints, shades, and saturation within a single color, puts the focus on value, and feels very unified.

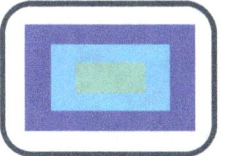

WARM COLOR
Warm colors are the family of colors ranging from yellows to reds. They remind the viewer of physically warm things like fire or sunlight.

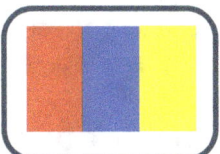

COOL COLOR
Cool colors are the family of colors ranging from blues to greens. They remind the viewer of physically cool things like water or ice.

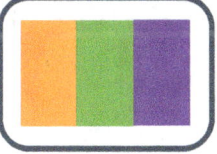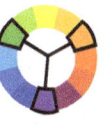

PRIMARY COLORS
Primary colors are the three colors that cannot be made by mixing. They form the foundation for all other colors and feel bright and vibrant.

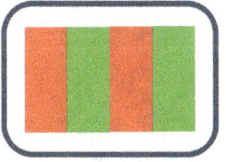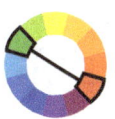

SECONDARY COLORS
Secondary colors are made by mixing two primary colors together. They feel less vibrant and more relaxed than primary colors.

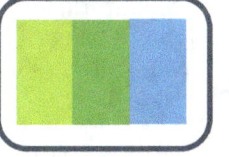

COMPLIMENTARY COLORS
Complimentary colors are those found on opposite sides of the color wheel. When placed together, they feel exciting and visually vibrate.

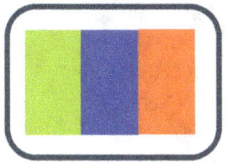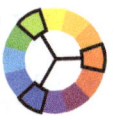

ANALOGOUS COLORS
Analogous colors are found next to each other on the color wheel and are easy to look at in relation to one another.

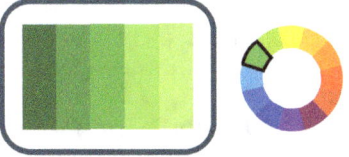

TRIADIC COLORS
Triadic colors are three colors equally spaced apart on the color wheel. They can feel harmonious despite being distant on the color wheel.

COLOR VARIATIONS

We think of colors as they relate to nomenclature but simply adding white or black, modifying saturation, or even putting a different color nearby can dramatically change the way we see them.

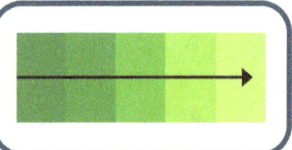

COLOR LUMINANCE: TINT (ADD WHITE)
Sometimes referred to as pastel, colors that have white added will often appear softer and more soothing.

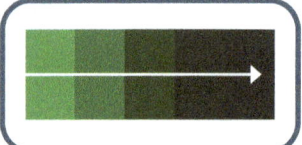

COLOR LUMINANCE: SHADE (ADD BLACK)
Adding black to a color will both darken and desaturate the color. Shades of colors often feel denser and even gloomy.

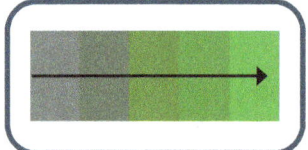

COLOR SATURATION (ADD PIGMENT)
The degree of saturation in a color is correlative to the amount of pigment present. Highly saturated colors are visual exciting.

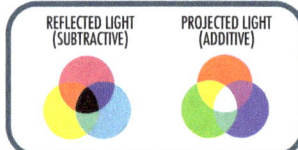

SUBTRACTIVE versus ADDITIVE COLOR
Subtractive color is reflected light with pigment absorbing light. Additive color is projected light with white being the projection of all colors.

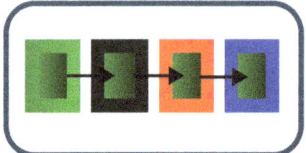

RELATIVE COLOR
We perceive colors differently based on their surroundings. Colors are more vibrant next to compliments and subdued next to analogs.

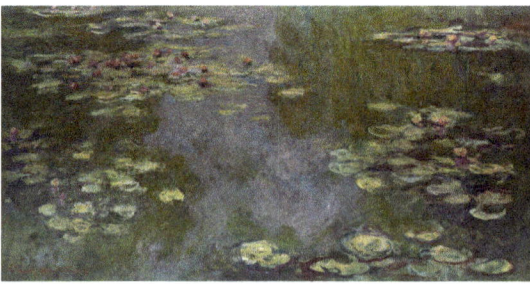

17. Claude Monet, *Water Lilies*, 1919

Claude Monet's painting of water lilies [figure 17] may appear monochromatic from a distance but upon closer inspection, he uses analogous colors to create a sense of harmony and complimentary colors to maintain visual excitement.

A much more active scene is depicted in Winslow Homer's 1910 painting [figure 18] which creates a feeling of excitement as the canoe speeds through the rapids. The red sash on the lead

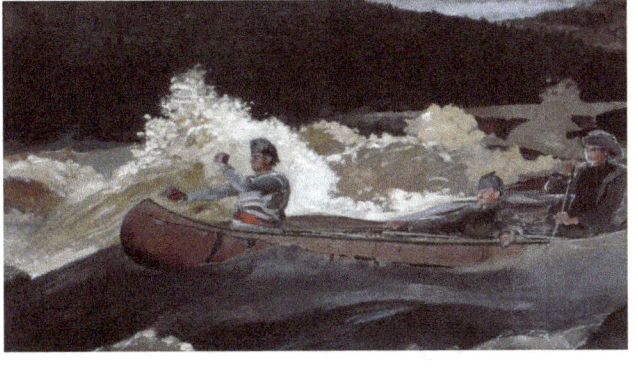

18. Winslow Homer, *Shooting the Rapids, Saguenay River*, 1905-10

figure is isolated from the color around it, reinforcing the movement and drama as the canoeists plunge forward.

APPLYING COMPOSITION PRINCIPLES TO COLOR

Arranging color can have incredible impacts on its perception, from increasing prominence with proportion to causing visual excitement by contrasting complimentary colors in close proximity.

BALANCE
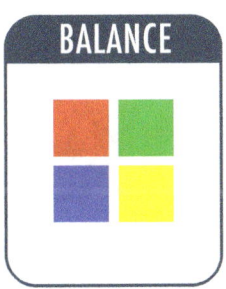

PROPORTION
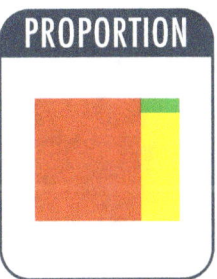

CONTRAST
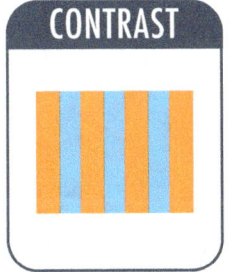

REPETITION
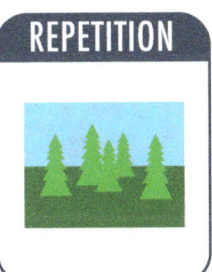

RHYTHM
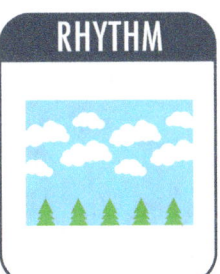

PATTERN
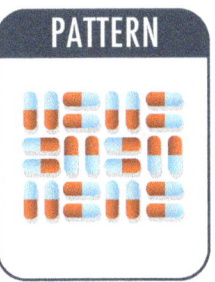

MOVEMENT
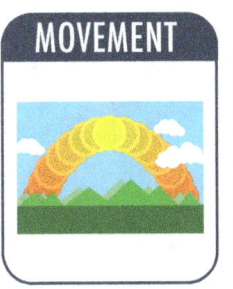

EMPHASIS
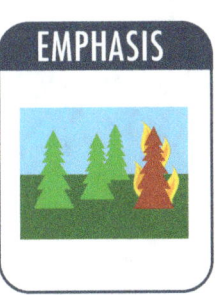

UNITY
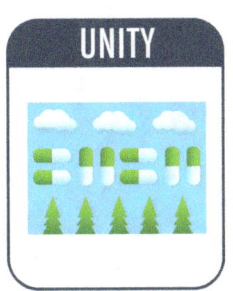

VARIETY
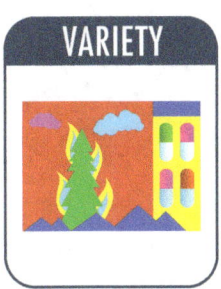

33

PART TWO

THE PRINCIPLES

THE ORGANIZATIONAL METHODS OF COMPOSITION

.

THE PRINCIPLES OF ART + DESIGN

If we imagine the elements of art and design as the ingredients in our magic potion of visual composition, then the principles are our cookbook of spells, dictating how and when we go about adding our ingredients to the potion. When selected for effect, elements and principles can work together to create powerful compositions that communicate with the viewer in ways that go beyond what content alone can accomplish. In their simplest form these combinations can act as a sort of equation. For example, low key value + jagged line x imbalance = scary. However, it is important to keep in mind that these combinations of elements and principles can also be extraordinarily complex and diffi cult to deploy in combination with the image's content in order to achieve a particular effect.

BALANCE

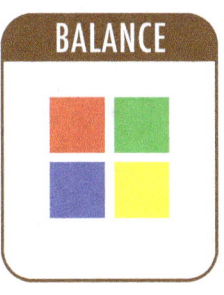

PROPORTION

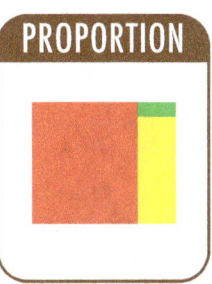

CONTRAST

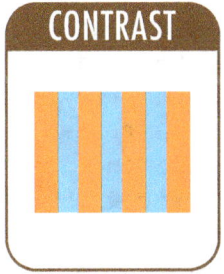

REPETITION

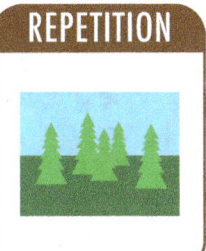

RHYTHM

PATTERN

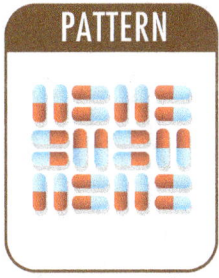

MOVEMENT

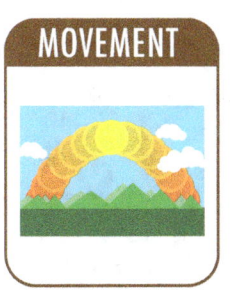

EMPHASIS

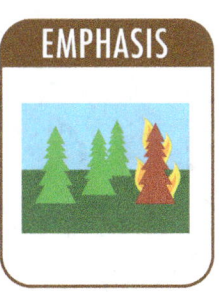

UNITY

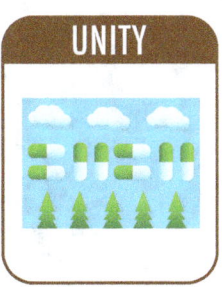

VARIETY

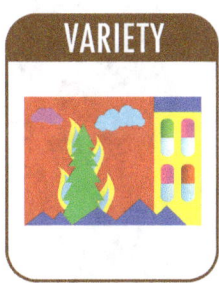

When used in combination with the elements of art and design, these organizing principles allow for the infinite combinations that we see when we walk through a museum, read a magazine, or play a video game. These compositions create more than just an image, they can dictate a viewer's experience of that image.

THE PRINCIPLES: BALANCE

At first it may seem strange to think of balance in the context of two-dimensional composition. After all, the substrate of the image whether paper or canvas is unlikely to be much heavier on one side than the other. However, it is the perception of visual weight that informs our sense of balance and this is predominately an effect of value and color. Darker values and more saturated colors appear heavier and changing their distribution in a composition can change the sense of balance or imbalance that is perceived by the viewer.

Balance is a visual principle that we closely relate to because our bodies are constantly in a state of balance or imbalance. The act of walking down a flight of stairs is really a series of controlled falls, constantly requiring the reacquisition of balance.

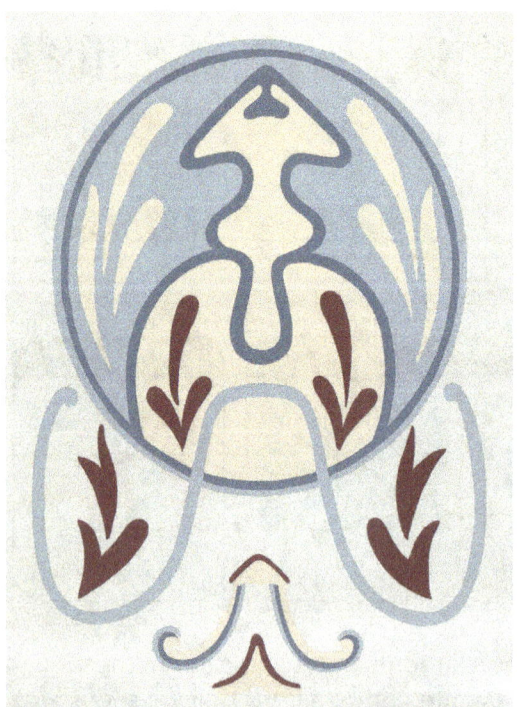

19. Unknown, *Wall Design - Asistencia of San Antonio de Pala* , 20th Century

In images, balance creates a feeling of stability and predictability when areas of an image have equal visual weight, either horizontally, vertically, or across the entire picture plane. Imbalance on the other hand creates a sense of instability and potentially even discomfort for the viewer.

In this 20th Century wall design [fi gure 19], the artist uses symmetrical balance to ground the image. Despite the upward movement that is created by the red and white teardrop shapes that fl ow toward the top of the design and the organic lines that support that upward movement, the image is quite stable due to its overall symmetry.

KINDS OF BALANCE

While we most often associate balance with symmetry, images can be asymmetrically balanced as well. A large dark area may be balanced by a cluster of smaller dark areas that are roughly equal in total dimension. Likewise, a large gray area may be balanced by an opposing small black area. Balance can also occur coaxially along both the vertical and horizontal axes, and even radially around a center point. We feel these symmetries or asymmetries in our bodies, and imagine the weight of the composition as a physical experience.

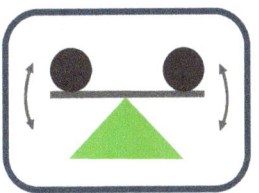

SYMMETRICAL BALANCE

In symmetrical balance the two sides of a composition are identical and thus have the same visual weight. Symmetrical balance can occur along any axis of a composition and creates a sense of stability.

ASYMMETRICAL BALANCE

Two sides of a composition can be balanced even when they are not identical by using differing components on each side of an axis that have similar visual weights, creating additional visual interest.

COAXIAL OR MULTIAXIAL BALANCE

Balance can occur along any axis of a composition and may also occur along multiple axes simultaneously. This multiaxial balance creates a sense of formality and even stasis in a composition.

RADIAL BALANCE

When components of a composition radiate out from a central point, it creates a kind of multiaxial balance called radial balance. This kind of balance is dynamic and can create a sense of outward movement or rotation.

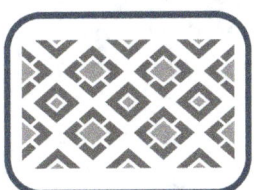

CRYSTALLOGRAPHIC BALANCE

When components are spread evenly across the entire composition creating an equal emphasis, it is known as crystallographic balance. This is often seen in conjunction with the elements of pattern and texture.

THE PRINCIPLES: PROPORTION

BALANCE

PROPORTION

CONTRAST

REPETITION

RHYTHM

PATTERN

MOVEMENT

EMPHASIS

UNITY

VARIETY

Proportion refers to perceived size relationships either within an image or between the viewer or surrounding architecture and the image itself. In the case of internal scale, we draw comparisons between the components within the image. We often think about these relationships in representational terms. For example, we have preconceived ideas about the size of fingers in relationship to the hand and deviations from this expectation can be disconcerting to the viewer.

Internal proportion may also refer to abstract components of a composition, with a one line being taller than another or a square being smaller than a circle. Additionally, we can consider proportion as the compositional component's relationship to the image. A component may dominate the composition by comprising a large portion of the picture frame.

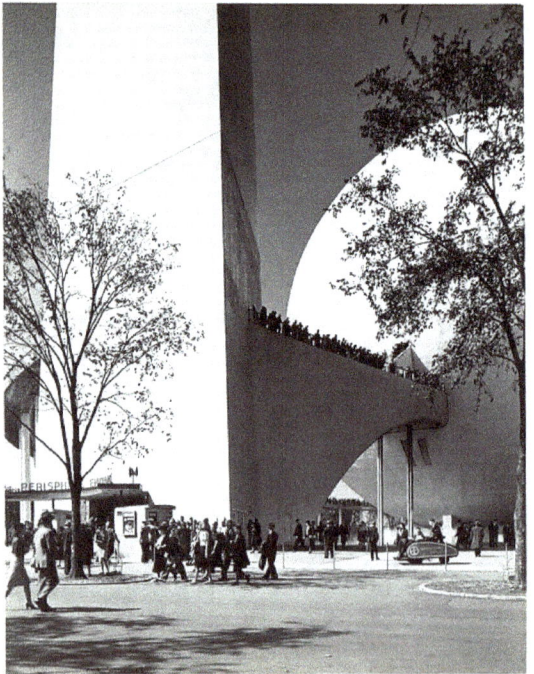

20. Samuel H. Gottscho, *1939 New York World's Fair, Entrance to Perisphere*, ca. 1939

In Samuel Gottscho's photograph of the entrance to the 1939 World's Fair [figure 20], he captures the scale of the architecture by deftly using proportion. The massive size of the architecture would be unclear even in relationship to the trees if not for the people lined up along the bridge to the enormous "Perisphere" which was 180 feet in diameter. Gottscho highlights the magnitude of the architecture by visually comparing it proportionally to the people in both the foreground and on the entryway bridge.

KINDS OF PROPORTION

While we often think of proportion as dealing with just the size relationship between elements within a composition, it can also refer to the size in relationship to the environment or the viewer. Proportion can be used to create dominant elements within a composition in order to emphasize those components. This principle can comfort us by holding to our expectations of how size relationships should work or deviate dramatically from those expectations in order to surprise us. Proportion can make us feel like giants or ants, can draw us into an intimate relationship with an image, or dominate a space.

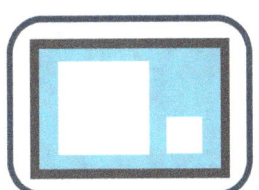

INTERNAL PROPORTION
The size relationship between elements within a composition is called internal proportion. The more contextual expectation we have for element size, the more dominant internal proportion becomes.

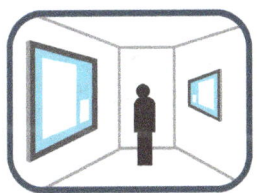

EXTERNAL PROPORTION
The size relationship between the viewer and the image or elements within the image is called external proportion. A small image may force an intimate engagement while a large image can feel monumental.

DOMINANT PROPORTION
A form of scale that utilizes our inclination toward hierarchy to emphasize elements based on size. Larger elements tend to be more dominant in relationship to smaller elements within the composition.

CONTINUAL PROPORTION
When we see the comparative size of elements within a composition repeat, we tend to predict that the relationship will remain the same even when both elements increase or decrease in size.

EXAGGERATIVE PROPORTION
Proportions can create a surreal experience for the viewer when they are dramatically different from our expectations. This exaggeration can feel whimsical or monstrous depending on context.

THE PRINCIPLES: CONTRAST

BALANCE
PROPORTION
▶ CONTRAST
REPETITION
RHYTHM
PATTERN
MOVEMENT
EMPHASIS
UNITY
VARIETY

Contrast calls attention to the dramatic differences between the components of an image. We most frequently associate contrast with the element of value and significant changes from light to dark within an image. When presented with the juxtaposition of light and dark within a composition, our attention gravitates to the place where the darkest and lightest values meet.

This same principle of attention holds true for other elements as well. For example, an image may seem to vibrate when colors from opposite sides of the color wheel are placed next to one another. When using highly saturated colors, these combinations can even be difficult for the viewer to look at for a sustained period.

John Henry Amschewitz's drawing of refugees [figure 21] uses value contrast to draw immediate attention to the faces of the two central figures in the composition, emphasizing their plight and ensuring that

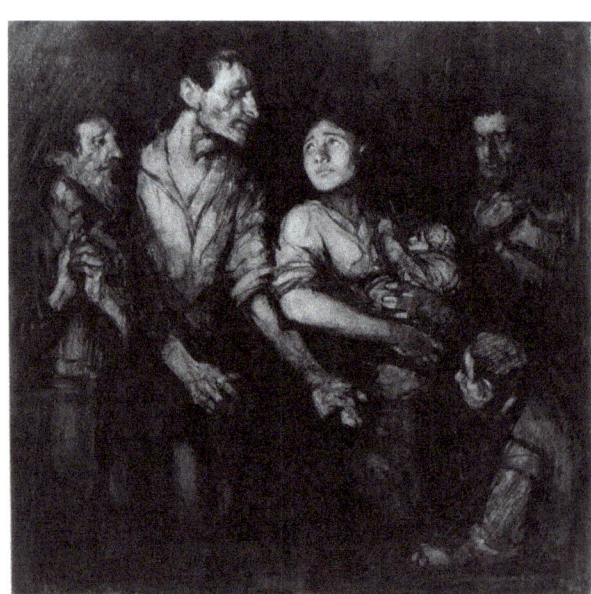

they are individuated through their expressions and not just seen as generalized entities. Though they are surrounded by other figures, the background behind the two central figures darkens significantly in comparison to the corners of the image, creating contrast in relationship to the stark white used in the faces. In comparison, the supporting figures fade into the background.

21. John Henry Amschewitz, *The Refugees*, ca. 1906

42

KINDS OF CONTRAST

There are a variety of elements beyond value that present opportunities to utilize dramatic differences to create excitement within a composition. For example, contrast may also refer to significant differences in the color, size, or even position of compositional components. It is important to note that the effects of contrast increase with proximity, so a high key and low key value will contrast sharply when next to one another but less so when seen in opposing corners of a composition.

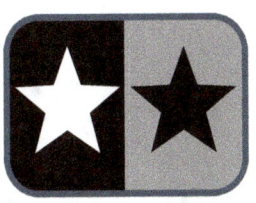

VALUE CONTRAST
When low key values are placed next to high key values, this creates contrast as our eye perceives the dramatic difference between the two.

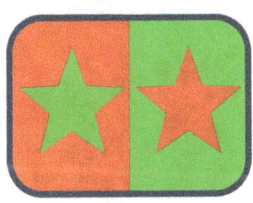

COLOR CONTRAST
Colors can contrast sharply when they come from opposing sides of the color wheel. These combinations are called "complimentary colors" and they are visually exciting and seem to vibrate.

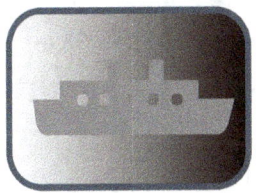

SIMULTANEOUS CONTRAST
Simultaneous contrast utilizes the surrounding value to create the illusion of value change. In this case the ship appears darker on the left and lighter on the right but is actually a single consistent value.

PROPORTIONAL CONTRAST
Differences in scale, especially when applied to like objects, creates proportional contrast. Think of a young David fighting the giant Goliath and the dramatic visual difference between the two.

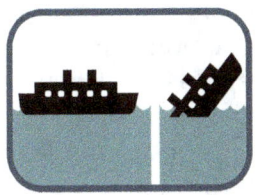

POSITIONAL CONTRAST
Positioning similar elements in very different ways can create dramatic relationships between them. In this instance we see that meaning is completely changed just by changing the position of the ship.

THE PRINCIPLES: REPETITION

Repetition refers to a repeated component within an image. Even when the components are not identical, the repeating of similar components can create a sense of motion or unify an image. We often find rhythm in compositions that utilize repetition and the combination can move the viewer's eye through the image at varying rates of speed. Repeated elements can also serve to emphasize a particular component within a complex image.

Repetition is commonly seen in our environment, from the windows and bricks of a building to the leaves on a tree. When not individuated, these repeated elements can generalize into a larger shape and make it less likely that we will inspect each instance of that shape carefully. For example, once we have examined one of the leaves on a tree, our assumption is that the rest are more or less the same.

In Paul Cezanne's still life [figure 22] we can see the form of the orange fruit is repeated numerous times which serves as both a unifying element of the composition and creates visual motion as our eye travels from each piece of fruit to the next. As demonstrated here, the fruit may be similar but not identical and still achieve repetition. In this painting, there are peaches, a lemon, and an apple but all have similar qualities in terms of shape and color.

22. Paul Cézanne, *Still Life with Milk Jug and Fruit*, ca. 1900

KINDS OF REPETITION

Andy Warhol said, "I like things to be exactly the same over and over again." Repeated elements encourage comparison of like objects and force our eye to follow from one element to the next, even when those elements only share slight similarities. Regular repetition can be comforting and infer the next beat in a steady rhythm whereas irregular repetition can feel unpredictable because we do not know what will happen next. This principle allows artists and designers to visually move the viewer through the composition, creating carefully ordered experiences. Repetition can also be used to reinforce ideas even when elements are visually different.

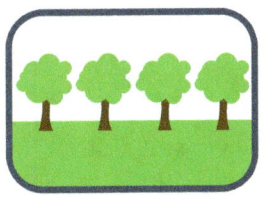

REGULAR REPETITION
Regular repetition may refer to both the rhythm of the repetition and the degree of similarity of the elements. For example, identical shapes presented at regular intervals feel formal and predictable.

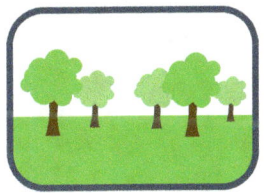

IRREGULAR REPETITION
When elements of a composition repeat but not at regular intervals, the repetition is considered irregular. Similarly, if the elements are similar but not identical, then irregularity is introduced to the repetition.

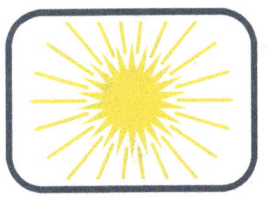

RADIAL REPETITION
Repetition around a central point produces a sense of rotation or divergent movement known as radial repetition.

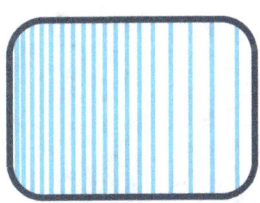

GRADIENT REPETITION
When an element changes gradually as it repeats, it creates gradient repetition. For example, a line may become increasingly thin, lighten, or grow closer together as it moves through the composition.

CONCEPTUAL REPETITION
Whether flowers or vehicles, some elements of a composition may share similar content while being visually disparate. This conceptual repetition serves to reinforce the shared idea of the repeated element.

THE PRINCIPLES: RHYTHM

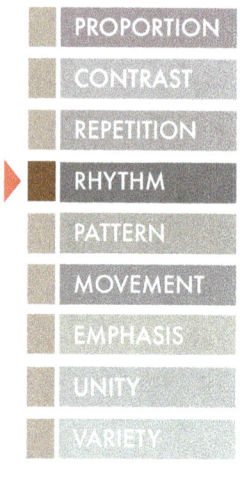

Rhythm in art and design is similar to rhythm in music or poetry in that it utilizes repeated elements to create a tempo that carries the viewer through the image. Rhythm and repetition go hand-in-hand, and without repetition it is virtually impossible to introduce rhythm into a composition.

Some rhythm is regular and easy to see, like a repeating pattern on wallpaper for instance. Other rhythm can be challenging to interpret because of the introduction of variations both in terms of the element that is being repeated and in the frequency of the repetition. Just as with music, rhythm in art and design can range from the tranquil to the chaotic. In the photograph *A Monday Washing* [figure 23] we see clothes hung out to dry between buildings in New York city around 1900. Though not identical, each piece of laundry and the lines themselves form an overlapping repetition that creates a sense of rhythm.

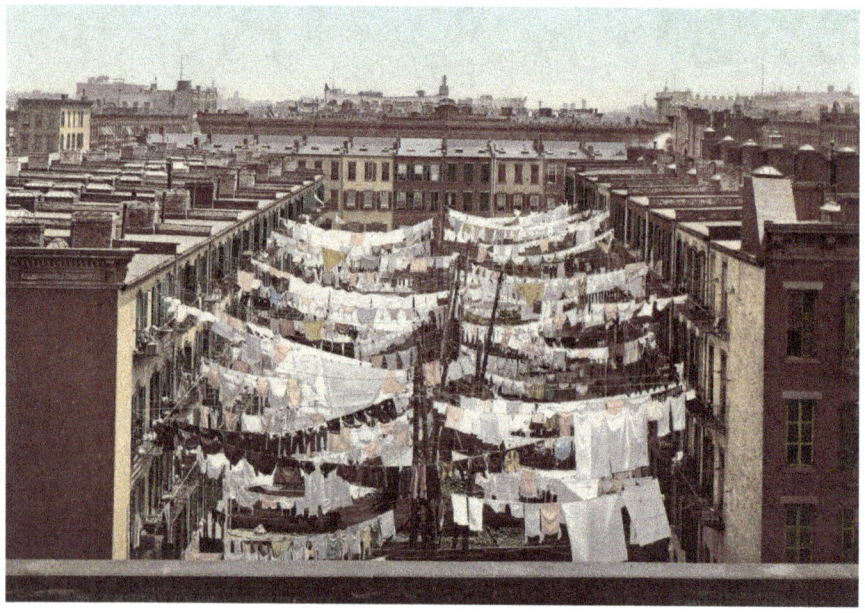

23. Unknown (Detroit Photographic Co.), *A Monday Washing, New York City*, 1900

KINDS OF RHYTHM

There are many ways in which we can arrange repeated elements in order to create the perception of rhythm. Regular rhythm is the easiest to discern because the constancy of its cadence produces a recognizable pattern. We can think of a regular rhythm as being like the steady beat of a marching drum. Irregular rhythm, on the other hand, is more difficult to see in a composition and can sometimes feel like a drum solo in a jazz song with the beat becoming tangible and then disappearing again into the complexities of the repeated compositional components.

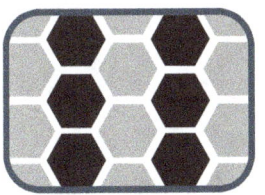

REGULAR RHYTHM

Regular rhythm is akin to the steady ticking of a clock. The regularity makes it easily discernible and can lead the viewer through the composition with a formal step-like progression.

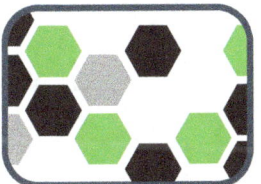

IRREGULAR RHYTHM

Unlike the steady repetition of regular rhythm, irregular rhythms feel more organic and free-flowing. Still reliant on repetition, this form of rhythm allows for significant variations to occur while still retaining some structure.

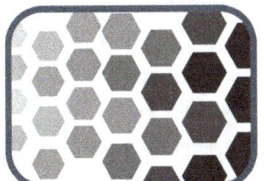

PROGRESSIVE RHYTHM

Progressive rhythm changes gradually as it spans a composition. Whether regular or irregular in structure, this rhythm is similar to gradient repetition with changes occurring as the rhythm progresses.

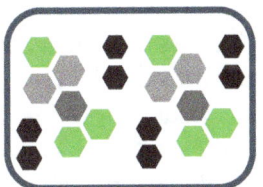

ALTERNATING RHYTHM

Alternating rhythms introduce pattern to the composition by moving back and forth between two distinct sub-rhythms. This is a common rhythm in music and creates visual interest while maintaining structure.

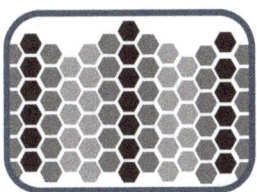

FLOWING OR UNDULATING RHYTHM

Combining the structure of alternating rhythm with the gradual changes found in progressive rhythm results in flowing or undulating rhythm as the rhythm alternated gradually between structures.

THE PRINCIPLES: PATTERN

BALANCE
PROPORTION
CONTRAST
REPETITION
RHYTHM
▶ PATTERN
MOVEMENT
EMPHASIS
UNITY
VARIETY

Pattern is all around us, from the way we structure speech to the clothing we wear, from the leaves on a tree to the cells that make up those leaves. Pattern emphasizes regularity through repetition and can incorporate a variety of elements into its framework. Regular patterns create visual interest and are often associated with visual texture.

Grids are the most common underlying structure for pattern and form the basis of many of the patterns we encounter. When thinking of grids, we may tend recall images of checkerboards or brick walls but grids are surprisingly common, from the alternating planks of a wood floor to the woven fibers that constitute much of our clothing. Grids are even found underlying the patterns on a snake's skin and in the construction of a bee hive.

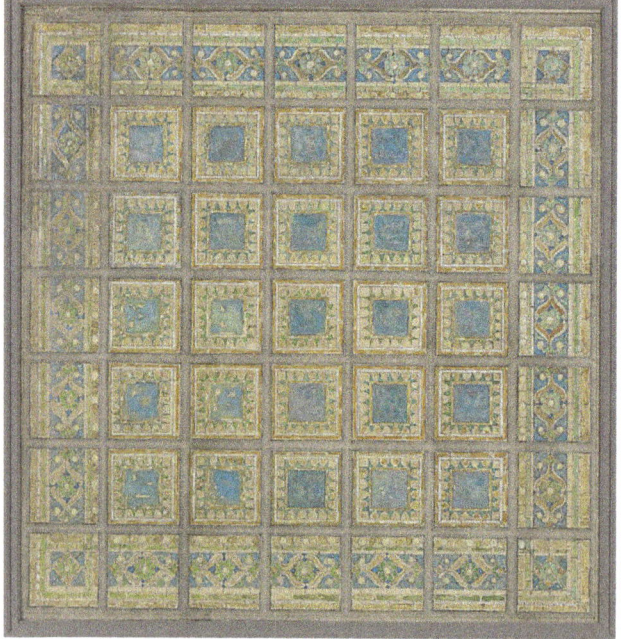

24. Louis Comfort Tiffany, *Design for Skylight Window*, 1902–32

This Tiffany design for a skylight [figure 24] incorporates a regular pattern that embraces the underlying structural grid and embellishes each square with intricate patterns in order to evoke a sense of opulence. The design incorporates warm analogous colors that unify the repeating squares and the outer squares incorporate a linear pattern that frames the interior.

KINDS OF PATTERN

Patterns in images can be subtle and supportive of other principles or bold and central to the image. Although they can form a consistently structural framework for other elements, they do vary in the kinds of framework that they provide. The grid is the most familiar underpinning structure but spirals and fractals can also provide structure for repeating pattern and are often seen in nature. For example, looking closely at the shapes found on a fern leaf reveal a fractal-based pattern while many shells incorporate spirals in their interior structures.

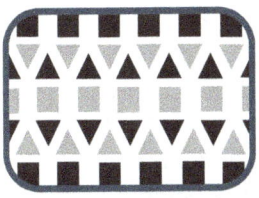

REGULAR PATTERN
Regular patterns provide significant structure for an image and can create a sense of predictability as the steady rhythms repeat sequentially.

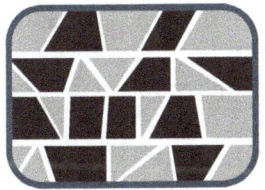

IRREGULAR PATTERN
Irregular patterns feel more organic and unpredictable as their repeating components change and shift. This can create visual excitement or become disconcerting if taken to extremes.

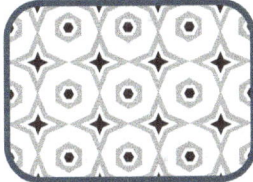

SEAMLESS PATTERN
Seamless patterns repeat endlessly without any discernible beginning or end. This kind of pattern is often seen in textile designs where bolts of fabric need to be printed without obvious breaks in the pattern.

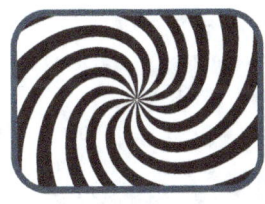

SPIRAL PATTERN
Commonly seen in nature, spiral patterns twirl around a point gradually converging toward their center. Spirals can create a strong sense of motion and are frequently associated with a feeling hypnosis or vertigo.

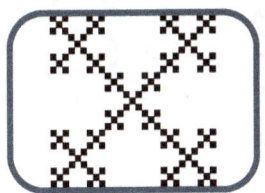

FRACTAL PATTERN
Fractals are patterns that repeat at varying scales, with each scale up or down being a reflection of the same pattern. Fractals are a common natural form and can also be created as images mathematically.

THE PRINCIPLES: MOVEMENT

BALANCE
PROPORTION
CONTRAST
REPETITION
RHYTHM
PATTERN
▶ MOVEMENT
EMPHASIS
UNITY
VARIETY

Movement in art and design may refer to either the movement of the eye across an image or the movement shown in the composition. Often working in combination, the optical movement of the eye can be accomplished by showing movement in the composition. Unlike showing movement in a film, depicting movement in a static image requires the artist to take into account the various ways in which we perceive movement.

While we are adept at following motion visually, a phenomenon called persistence of vision allows us to also see movement when presented with a stream of images in rapid succession. This is why we see films as fluid motion despite being a series of projected images and why you can see through your hand when you wave it rapidly in front of your eyes. Artists working with static images have to rely on the implication of movement to force our minds to imagine the moment before and the moment after the frozen frame that the viewer sees.

Claude Monet uses this implication of movement in *The Green Wave*

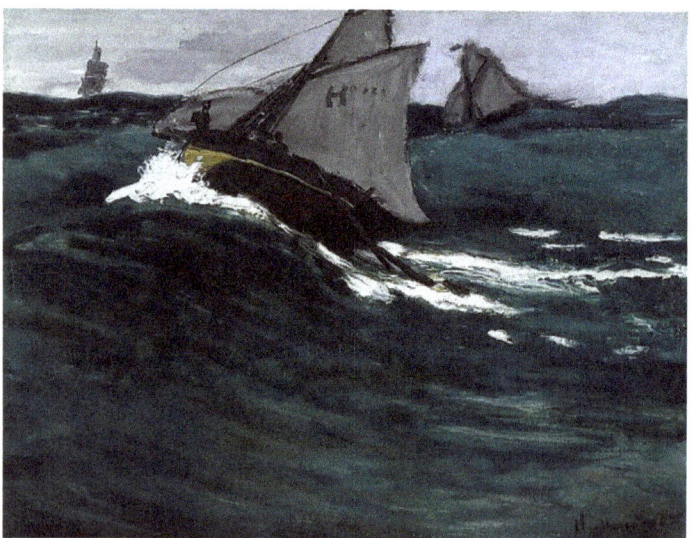

[figure 25]. The sailboat careens over the wave with a trail of bright white in its wake and a crash of white foam at the bow, giving us both an indication of the boat's previous location and indicating its direction.

25. Claude Monet, *The Green Wave*, ca. 1866–67

KINDS OF MOVEMENT

Both optical and perceptual types of movement engage the viewer in the action and move their eyes around the composition, creating an active viewing scenario. The viewer cannot help but imagine the past and future position of an element or to follow a series of similar components around a composition like breadcrumbs through the forest. Movement creates a dynamic viewing experience and can be deployed to construct narratives and purposefully lead the viewer through the composition.

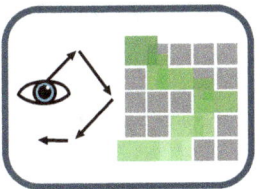

DYNAMIC OPTICAL MOVEMENT
Using gradual changes in visual components located near one another within the composition drives the eye fluidly from one element to the next creating dynamic motion.

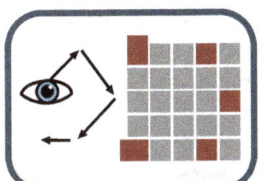

STATIC OPTICAL MOVEMENT
Static optical movement relies on the viewer's tendency to see one like element and then visually jump to another, like following breadcrumbs.

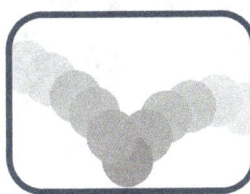

PERCEPTUAL MOVEMENT
Movement can be portrayed in ways that mirror our limited capacity to perceive rapid motion by showing a "ghost" of the element's previous position.

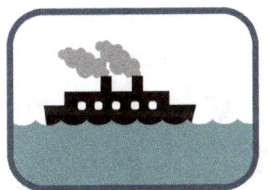

IMPLIED MOVEMENT
We can give a sense of the movement to an element or object based on what surrounds it. For instance, dirt flying from the hooves of a horse or a dandelion seeds being blown into the air by a breeze shows movement.

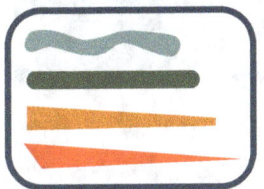

VELOCITY MOVEMENT
Ever wonder why sports cars are red, angular, and get more speeding tickets? Warm shapes appear faster than cool shapes and acutely angular shapes seem faster than rounded or even obtusely angular shapes.

THE PRINCIPLES: EMPHASIS

Emphasis occurs when one element of an image appears more prominent than others. This draws particular attention to the emphasized element and gives the image a focal point. Often this is accomplished by making the component significantly different from the others in the composition in order to call attention to it. Compositional components that are anomalous in their surroundings stand apart and capture the viewer's attention.

In Rembrandt van Rijn's painting *The Mill* [figure 26] the windmill is the obvious focal point of the painting. He accomplishes this tight focus by isolating the windmill from its surroundings using high contrast value with the dark windmill set against the bright sky, deploying color on the windmill that does not appear elsewhere in the painting, and using geometric shapes that stand apart from the organic shapes in the surrounding landscape.

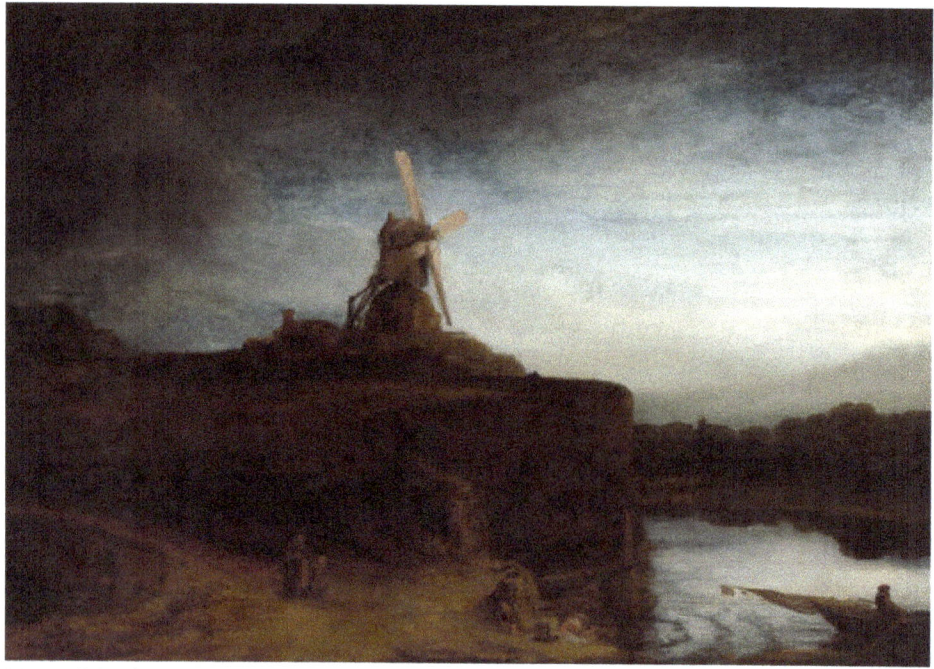

26. Rembrandt van Rijn, *The Mill*, 1645/1648

KINDS OF EMPHASIS

Artists and designers often use emphasis to draw attention to particular focal points within a composition. Emphasis can be invoked by something that seems out of place or breaks with our expectations. It may be an element that is in some small way different from elements that are otherwise similar or created by something that is completely separate from its surroundings. Emphasis can even be accomplished by the convergence of components within the composition. Emphasis allows the artist or designer to create a strong focal point even within complex images.

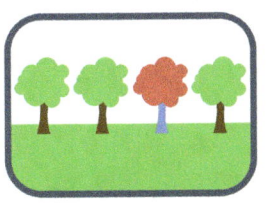

ANOMALOUS EMPHASIS
When a compositional element is significantly different than the rest of the composition, especially if it also differs from our expectations, it is emphasized by being anomalous.

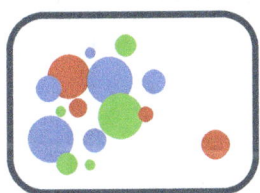

ISOLATION EMPHASIS
Elements that are isolated from their surroundings are easily seen compared to those that are jumbled together. This isolation may be accomplished in a variety of ways including position, color, and value.

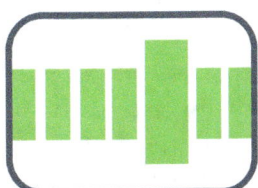

PROPORTIONAL EMPHASIS
Compositional elements can be emphasized by being made significantly different in size than the other elements within the composition.

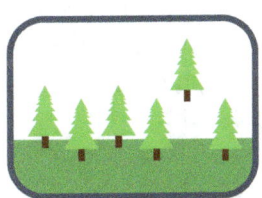

POSITIONAL EMPHASIS
Putting an element in a different position than other like elements within the composition can result in emphasis. Here, raising the element higher than the rest makes it more prominent.

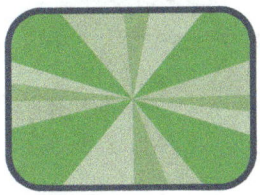

CONVERGENCE EMPHASIS
When elements converge in an area of the composition it can emphasize the place where the convergence occurs, drawing our eye to the moment of intersection.

THE PRINCIPLES: UNITY

BALANCE
PROPORTION
CONTRAST
REPETITION
RHYTHM
PATTERN
MOVEMENT
EMPHASIS
UNITY
VARIETY

Unity brings similar elements together and can either be applied to one aspect of an image or the image as a whole. Unified images feel harmonious and have more focus on the sum of their parts than on the individual components that comprise them. Unity within the bounds of a picture or internal unity will bring elements into a group so that they are seen as a whole. Unity of the entire image causes the viewer to see the image first as a unified whole before focusing on the individual components within the composition.

The idea of designing images with the goal of the viewer perceiving them as a unified whole dates back to a group of German psychologists in the 1920's who developed a theory of visual perception called Gestalt Theory. The concepts behind Gestalt are closely related to the principle of unity, especially as it applies to the whole image rather than its constituent parts.

In Childe Hassam's 1913 impressionist painting *Surf, Isle of Shoals,* [figure 27] he utilizes color, mark making, and repetition to create an image that reads first as a unified whole. We can imagine the repeating pattern

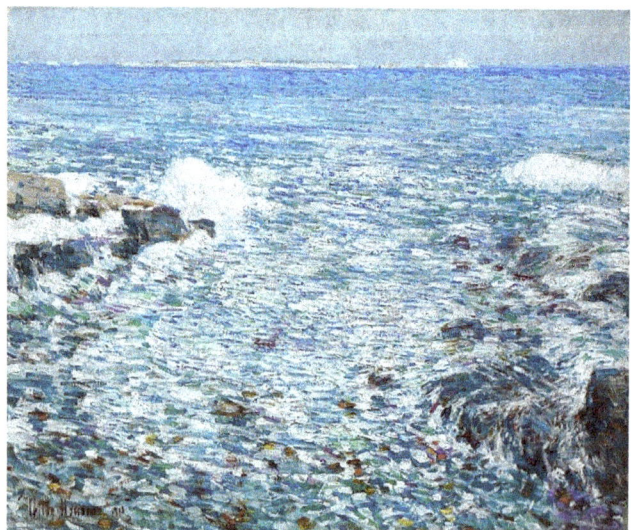

of blues and greens extending rhythmically to the distant horizon. The color and mark are consistent to the point of almost being hypnotic and framed by a few rocks introduced in the foreground, the center of the composition invites the viewer to follow the rhythmic blue marks to the horizon.

27. Childe Hassam, *Surf, Isle of Shoals*, 1913

KINDS OF UNITY

Unity can be achieved either through the use of similar elements or the positioning of elements in certain ways. As noted, unity may apply to the whole image and rely on similarities of the elements used throughout or may apply to just a portion of the image. Often when unity is applied to various areas of a composition it will result in a more unified whole. The danger in the creation of highly unified images is that they can become monotonous. The introduction of too many similar elements can result in an extreme predictability that has the potential to lose visual interest.

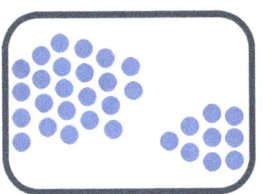

PROXIMAL UNITY
Elements appear to be part of a whole when they are clustered together. We can imagine groups of people in a crowded space and how we might identify those who are clustered together as part of a social group.

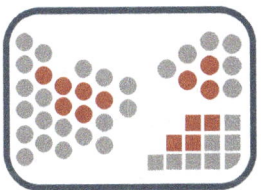

SIMILAR UNITY
We can imagine that same crowded space with clusters of people but now envision that some of them are wearing a red uniform. Now we are more likely to see those similarly dressed people as part of a group.

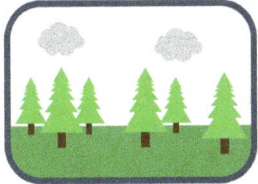

REPETITIOUS UNITY
Repetition using many of the same elements tends to unify an image. When like elements appear throughout a composition those elements tie the composition together through their similarity.

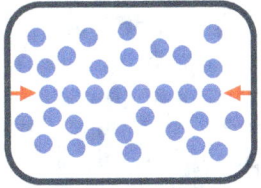

POSITIONAL UNITY
When elements align we see them as part of a group or a single unit. For example, when a series of elements aligns along a single axis we see those elements as part of a whole or grouping.

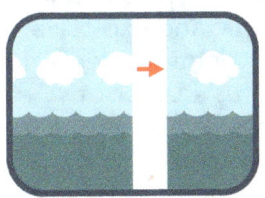

CONTINUAL UNITY
When composition demonstrates a strong sense of repetition within the bounds of the picture frame we are inclined to imagine that repetition going on and on beyond the image.

THE PRINCIPLES: VARIETY

BALANCE
PROPORTION
CONTRAST
REPETITION
RHYTHM
PATTERN
MOVEMENT
EMPHASIS
UNITY
▶ VARIETY

Variety is the spice of life or so the saying goes and when applied to visual compositions variety adds visual interest by breaking monotony. Surprisingly, as with it's opposite unity, when variety is taken to excess it likewise runs the risk of becoming monotonous because everything is equally different.

Variety is often thought of in terms of adding visually dissimilar elements into a composition but in fact it can be achieved through changes to position and adding elements that do not seem to belong together conceptually. The latter is sometimes employed in scenarios where the viewer is intended to question the inclusion of a particular element within a composition.

In Wassily Kandinsky's *Kleine Welten I* [figure 28] we find an array of elements, very few of which are similar. This creates a playful, whimsical feeling image that invites the viewer to pay more attention to the

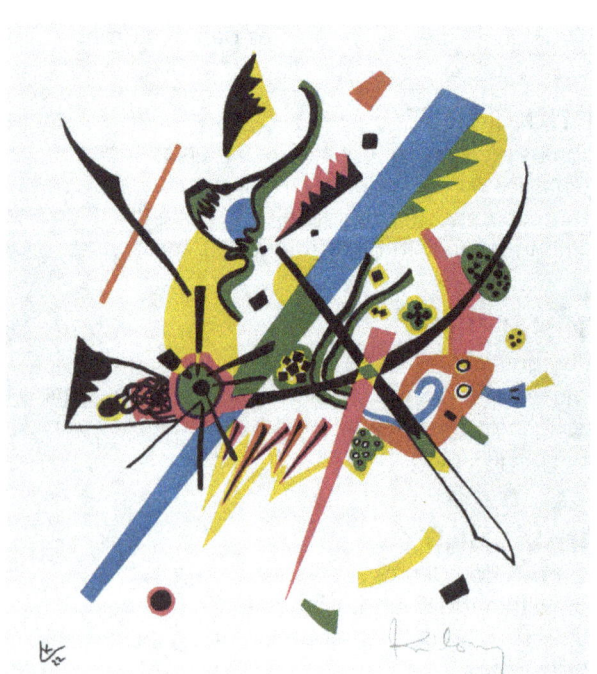

individual elements than to the image as a whole. The diagonal blue bar slices the image into two diagonal halves while the smallest components float around the outside of the composition like confetti. Some lines are calligraphic while others are angular and pointed. The cluster of shapes in the middle of the composition feel chaotic and explosive. The variety of elements creates a sense of unpredictability and excitement.

28. Wassily Kandinsky, *Kleine Welten I (Small Worlds I)*, 1922

KINDS OF VARIETY

Dissimilarity is central to creating variety. Components of a composition that break from regularity and force the viewer to consider each element as individual or unique create visually engaging scenarios. Excessive uniformity in an image can lead to a lack of visual energy which is why variety is often used to break compositional monotony and generate visual excitement. Whether introducing unexpected positioning, dissimilar elements, or compositional anomalies, variety can be particularly useful when trying to visually communicate chaos or excess to an audience.

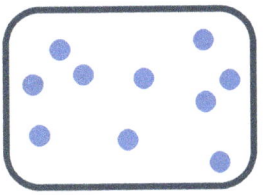

POSITIONAL VARIETY
Though components of a composition may be similar or even identical, they can be varied simply by causing their position to be unpredictable and arrhythmic.

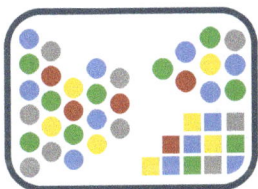

DISSIMILAR VARIETY
As seen in Kandinsky's *Kleine Welten I*, the inclusion of elements that are dissimilar in nature creates variety and generates visual excitement and unpredictability.

ANOMALOUS VARIETY
Variety can create emphasis when the dissimilar element that is introduced is surrounded by more homogeneous, expected elements.

CONTRAST VARIETY
Introducing contrasting or opposing elements creates a discordant note and calls attention to the differences between compositional components, making them feel more individuated.

CONCEPTUAL VARIETY
Components of a composition that do not readily connect conceptually can create variety in a composition causing the viewer to question the relationships of the elements.

PART THREE

EXERCISES
ANALYSIS USING THE ELEMENTS AND PRINCIPLES OF ART & DESIGN

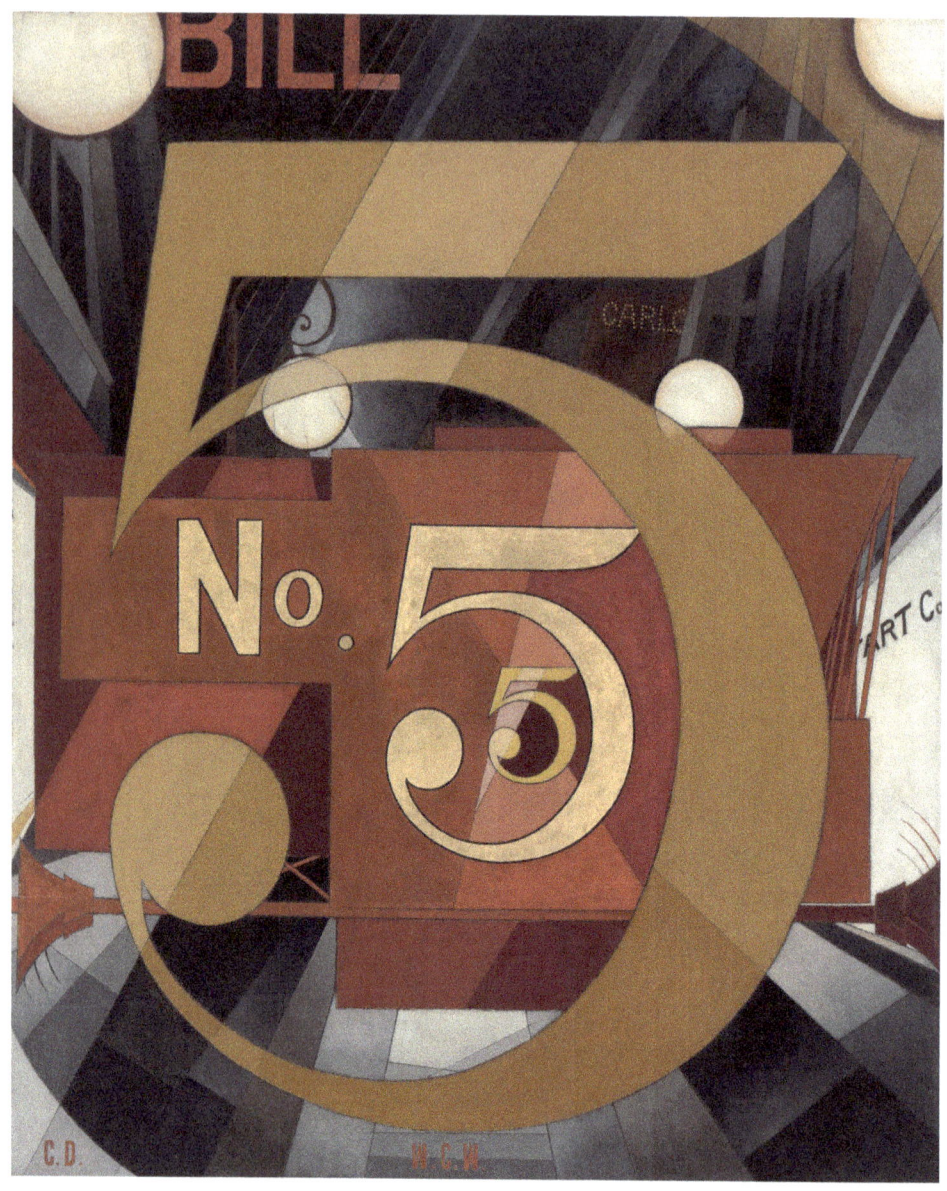

29. Charles Demuth, *I Saw the Figure 5 in Gold*, 1928

This 1928 painting by Charles Demuth [figure 29] is an homage to a poem by his friend William Carlos Williams about a fire engine rushing through the streets of New York City to the scene of a fire. Demuth uses a variety of elements and principles to portray both the speed and the noise of the fire engine as it rushes by.

EXERCISE 1: MOTION AND SOUND

What does the artist use to depict both the motion and the sound of the fire engine speeding through the New York City streets? Analyze the image to see how the elements and principles of art and design are contributing to the feeling of the artwork.

HOW DOES THE ARTWORK FEEL?

_____

ELEMENTS

Which elements are most prominent in creating the overall feeling of the artwork?

1 _____

2 _____

3 _____

4 _____

5 _____

6 _____

☑

- [ ] POINT
- [ ] LINE
- [ ] SHAPE
- [ ] VALUE
- [ ] FORM
- [ ] TEXTURE
- [ ] SPACE
- [ ] COLOR

PRINCIPLES

Which principles contribute to the overall feeling of the artwork?

1 _____

2 _____

3 _____

4 _____

5 _____

6 _____

7 _____

☑

- [ ] BALANCE
- [ ] PROPORTION
- [ ] CONTRAST
- [ ] REPETITION
- [ ] RHYTHM
- [ ] PATTERN
- [ ] MOVEMENT
- [ ] EMPHASIS
- [ ] UNITY
- [ ] VARIETY

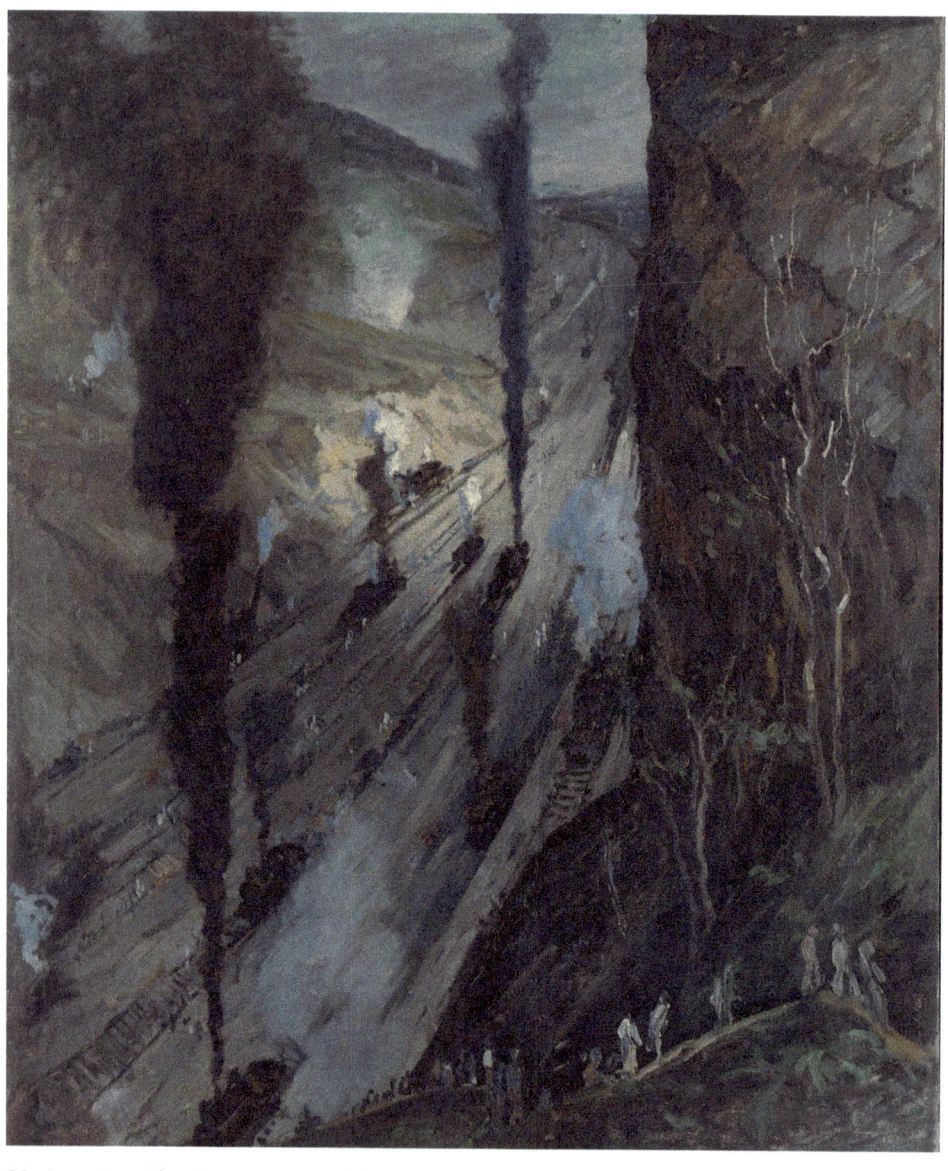

30. Jonas Lie, *The Conquerors (Culebra Cut, Panama Canal)*, 1913

In 1913, Jonas Lie visited the Panama Canal construction site and created numerous depictions of the massive endeavor [figure 30]. Known as an artist, poet, and even scientist for his studies of New York City, the Norwegian-born painter was captivated by the monumental scale of the project and its technical complexity, a fascination which he translated into the thirty known paintings produced from the trip.

EXERCISE 2: MONUMENTAL SIZE

Which elements and principles contribute to the monumental feeling of this image of the Panama Canal construction project? How does the artist portray the impressive speed of the canal's progress?

HOW DOES THE ARTWORK FEEL?

ELEMENTS

Which elements are most prominent in creating the overall feeling of the artwork?

☑

1 _____
2 _____
3 _____
4 _____
5 _____
6 _____

☐ POINT
☐ LINE
☐ SHAPE
☐ VALUE
☐ FORM
☐ TEXTURE
☐ SPACE
☐ COLOR

PRINCIPLES

Which principles contribute to the overall feeling of the artwork?

☑

1 _____
2 _____
3 _____
4 _____
5 _____
6 _____
7 _____

☐ BALANCE
☐ PROPORTION
☐ CONTRAST
☐ REPETITION
☐ RHYTHM
☐ PATTERN
☐ MOVEMENT
☐ EMPHASIS
☐ UNITY
☐ VARIETY

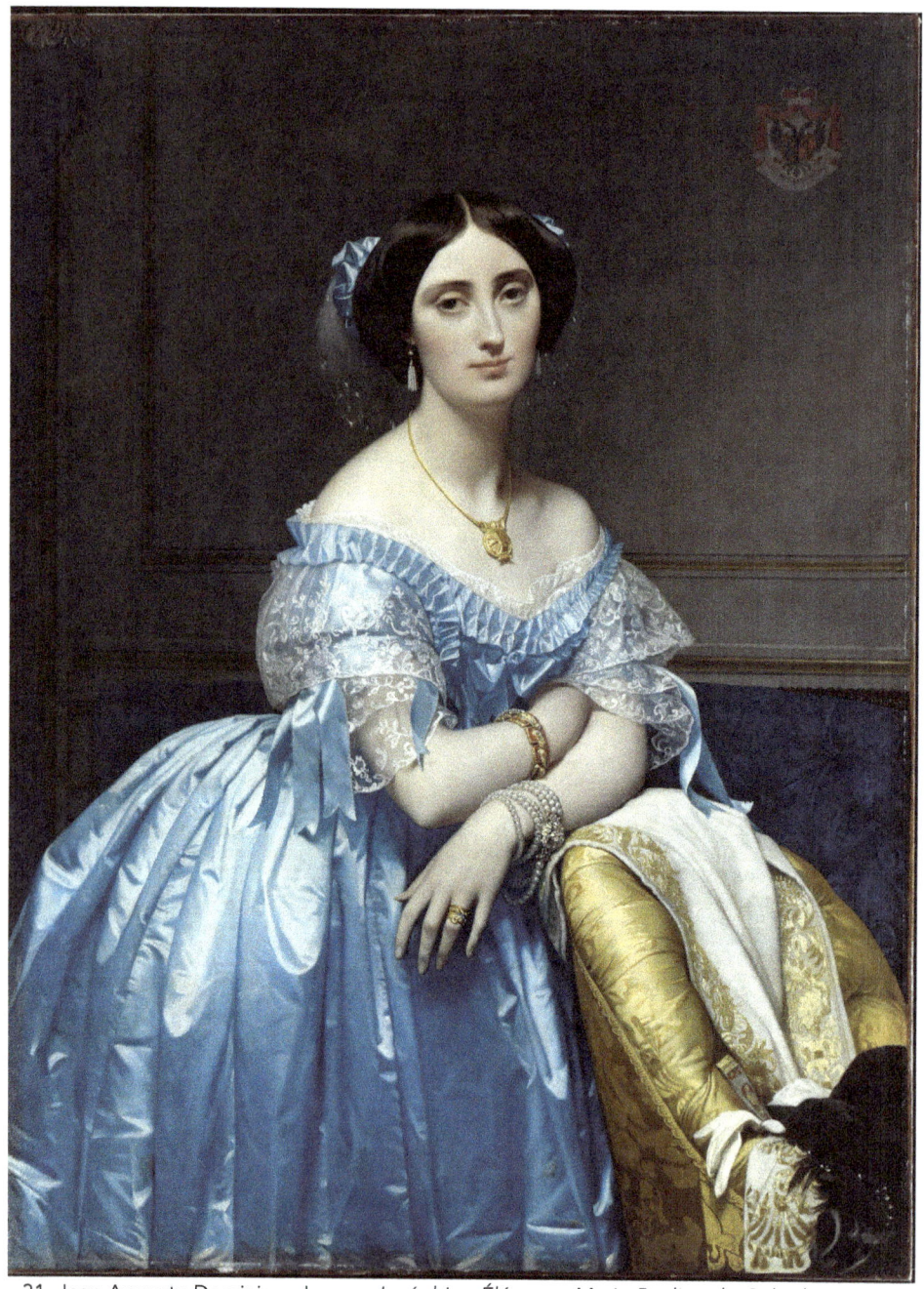

31. Jean Auguste Dominique Ingres, *Joséphine-Éléonore-Marie-Pauline de Galard de Brassac de Béarn (1825–1860), Princesse de Broglie* 1851-53

In the final painting commission of Jean-Auguste-Dominique Ingres' life, the artist created a tour de force showcase of his ability to portray opulence with near photographic treatments of expensive fabrics [figure 31].

EXERCISE 3: CREATING OPULENCE

Ingres uses both elements and principles to demonstrate not only his extraordinary painting skill but also to tell the story of the subject's wealth. How does the artist portray the opulence of the subject despite her apparently reserved demeanor?

HOW DOES THE ARTWORK FEEL?

ELEMENTS

Which elements are most prominent in creating the overall feeling of the artwork?

1 _____

2 _____

3 _____

4 _____

5 _____

6 _____

☑

- [ ] POINT
- [ ] LINE
- [ ] SHAPE
- [ ] VALUE
- [ ] FORM
- [ ] TEXTURE
- [ ] SPACE
- [ ] COLOR

PRINCIPLES

Which principles contribute to the overall feeling of the artwork?

1 _____

2 _____

3 _____

4 _____

5 _____

6 _____

7 _____

☑

- [ ] BALANCE
- [ ] PROPORTION
- [ ] CONTRAST
- [ ] REPETITION
- [ ] RHYTHM
- [ ] PATTERN
- [ ] MOVEMENT
- [ ] EMPHASIS
- [ ] UNITY
- [ ] VARIETY

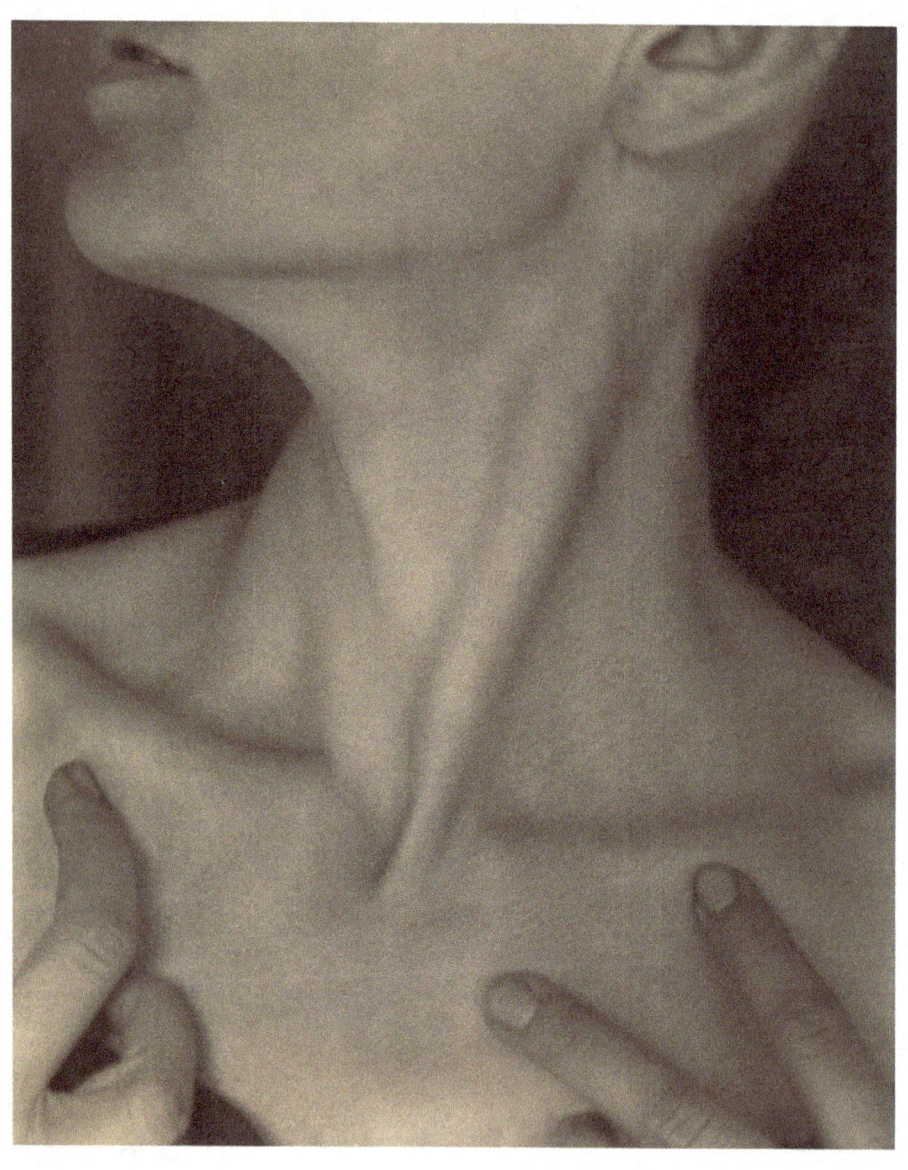

32. Alfred Stieglitz, *Georgia O'Keeffe — Neck*, 1921

Taken five years after they met and three years before they were married, this portrait of the painter Georgia O'Keeffe by renowned photographer Alfred Stieglitz [figure 32] is one of more than three hundred photographs he made of her over a twenty year period. The portrait demands intimacy of the viewer by not showing her face and instead focusing solely on the neck. Stieglitz's use of form reflects the sensuousness of newly found desire.

EXERCISE 4: PASSION AND DESIRE

How does Stieglitz's photograph of Georgia O'Keeffe reveal passion and desire using the elements and principles of art and design? What does he use to ensure that the portrait feels intimate to the viewer in ways that a traditional portrait might not?

HOW DOES THE ARTWORK FEEL?

ELEMENTS

Which elements are most prominent in creating the overall feeling of the artwork?

1 _____

2 _____

3 _____

4 _____

5 _____

6 _____

☑
- [ ] POINT
- [ ] LINE
- [ ] SHAPE
- [ ] VALUE
- [ ] FORM
- [ ] TEXTURE
- [ ] SPACE
- [ ] COLOR

PRINCIPLES

Which principles contribute to the overall feeling of the artwork?

1 _____

2 _____

3 _____

4 _____

5 _____

6 _____

7 _____

☑
- [ ] BALANCE
- [ ] PROPORTION
- [ ] CONTRAST
- [ ] REPETITION
- [ ] RHYTHM
- [ ] PATTERN
- [ ] MOVEMENT
- [ ] EMPHASIS
- [ ] UNITY
- [ ] VARIETY

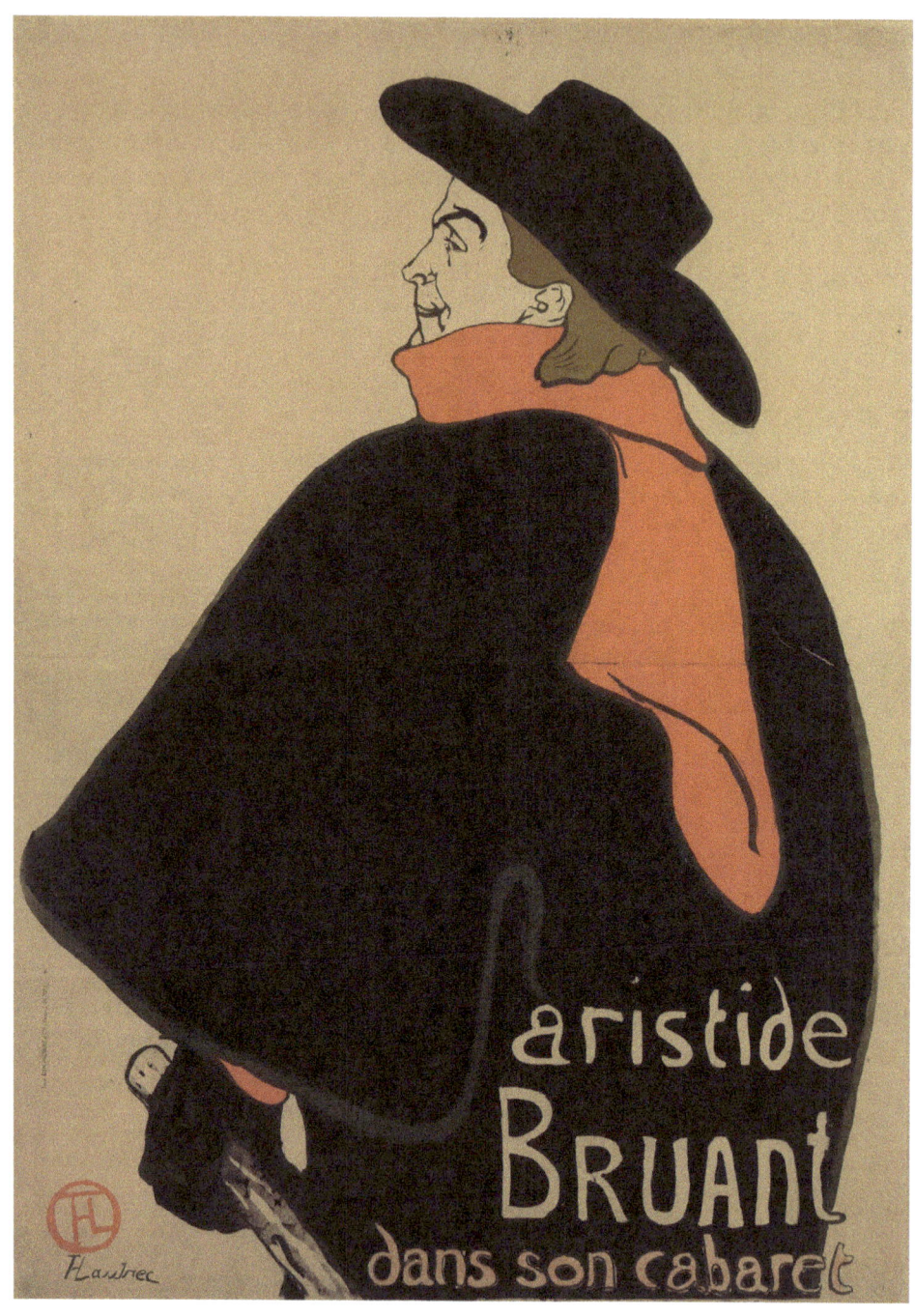

33. Henri de Toulouse-Lautrec, *Aristide Bruant, at His Cabaret*, 1893

When performer and songwriter Aristide Bruant hired Lautrec to design a poster to promote him, Lautrec used Braunt's signature costume to create an exciting graphic image that captured the attention of passersby [figure 33].

EXERCISE 5: THE POWER TO CAPTIVATE

Which elements and principles does Lautrec use to ensure that the viewer passing on a busy street will notice the image from afar while still retaining enough visual interest to engage the viewer up close?

HOW DOES THE ARTWORK FEEL?

ELEMENTS

Which elements are most prominent in creating the overall feeling of the artwork?

☑

☐	POINT
☐	LINE
☐	SHAPE
☐	VALUE
☐	FORM
☐	TEXTURE
☐	SPACE
☐	COLOR

1 _____

2 _____

3 _____

4 _____

5 _____

6 _____

PRINCIPLES

Which principles contribute to the overall feeling of the artwork?

☑

☐	BALANCE
☐	PROPORTION
☐	CONTRAST
☐	REPETITION
☐	RHYTHM
☐	PATTERN
☐	MOVEMENT
☐	EMPHASIS
☐	UNITY
☐	VARIETY

1 _____

2 _____

3 _____

4 _____

5 _____

6 _____

7 _____